15

MINUTES

ALONE WITH GOD

FOR MEN

BOB BARNES

HARVEST HOUSE PUBLISHERS
EUGENE, OREGON

Cover design by Knail, Salem, Oregon

Cover photo © Nicklas Blom / plainpicture / Matton

15 MINUTES ALONE WITH GOD FOR MEN
Copyright © 1995 by Bob Barnes
Published 2014 by Harvest House Publishers
Eugene, Oregon 97402
www.harvesthousepublishers.com

ISBN 978-0-7369-5389-4 (pbk.)
ISBN 978-0-7369-5390-0 (eBook)

Barnes, Bob.
    15 minutes alone with God for men / Bob Barnes.
        p. cm.
    ISBN 978-0-7369-1083-5 (pbk.)
    1. Men—Prayer-books and devotions—English. I. Title.
    II. Title: Fifteen minutes alone with God for men.
    BV4843.B37 1995
    242'.642—dc20

                                                                94-44254

Printed in the United States of America

17 18 19 20 21 22 / VP-JH / 10 9 8 7 6

*To the various pastors, coaches, businessmen, and
fellow journeyers who have contributed to my Christian walk.
Though you are far too many to mention by name,
I have been blessed through the years by your
guidance, love, and example.*

*I especially want to dedicate this devotional to
my son, Bradley, his two sons, Bradley Joe II and Weston;
my two other grandsons, Chad and Bevan Merrihew;
my son-in-law, Bill Whitney, and my grandson-in-law, Pat Ianni.
You certainly contribute to the goodness of my life!
May you all stay near to God so that
He will impact your lives in a mighty way.*

From Bob

Each decade introduces new challenges for men. We now find ourselves faced with more distractions, temptations, diversions, and opportunities than ever. So plentiful and frequent are the choices spinning in front of us, that many of us struggle to get off the merry-go-round long enough to spend time with God. The absence of that important time can lead to a life of hurried decisions, anxious thoughts, and uncertainty—even fear—about our future and our purpose.

One thing I've learned during my lifetime is to be purposeful in all I do. There are so many choices that seem good, but they don't energize me to become the man God created me to be. How wonderful that we can choose to pause and refresh our minds, thoughts, spirits, and hearts by asking, "Why am I here on earth? Who does God call me to be?"

My hope is that your identity as a godly man will become clearer and more compelling as you spend time immersed in these readings, key Scripture verses, prayers, and action steps. There are three boxes in the top corner of each entry. Because these devotions can be read in any order and will help you more than once, you can put check marks in the boxes to track your progress. The material in this devotional is designed to challenge and encourage you in your spiritual journey by daily reading Scripture and meditations built around the verses. It takes twenty-one days to develop a new habit. And unlike many of life's distractions, this habit—this choice—can transform your life, marriage, relationships, perspective, and faith in amazing and eternal ways.

Let's begin together.

Bob Barnes

Time for God

SCRIPTURE READING: Psalm 116:1-2

KEY VERSE: Psalm 116:2
I will call on [the LORD] as long as I live.

You know you should spend time with God each day, but have you ever really considered what God wants to give you during those daily times with Him? The apostle Paul wrote, "The fruit of the Spirit is love, joy, peace, patience, kindness, goodness, faithfulness, gentleness, self-control" (Galatians 5:22-23 NASB). These—along with guidance, wisdom, hope, and a deeper knowledge of Him—are what God wants to give to us, His children. Think about each item in Paul's list. Which of us doesn't need a touch of God's love, patience, kindness, goodness, gentleness, and self-control in our life?

"But," you say, "who has time? My to-do list is always longer than my day. I run from the time the alarm goes off in the morning until I fall into bed at night. How can I possibly find time to do one more thing? When could I find even a few minutes to read the Bible or pray?" Let me answer your questions with a question: Are you doing what's important in your day—or only what is urgent?

People do what they want to do. All of us make choices, and when we don't make time for God in our day, when we don't make time for the most important relationship in our lives, we are probably not making the *best* choices.

God greatly desires to spend time alone with you. After all, you are His child (John 1:12; Galatians 3:26). He created you, He loves you, and He gave His only Son for your salvation. Your heavenly Father wants to know you, and He wants you to know Him. The Creator of the universe wants to meet with you alone daily. How can you say no to such an opportunity?

I know people who spend hours commuting on the California freeways and use that time to be with God. I used to pray while I was driving an hour between home and work. Now that our children are raised and our home is quiet, I find mornings—before the telephone starts to ring or I get involved in the day's activities—are the best times for me to be alone with God. And I love getting to church early and having 10 or 15 minutes to open my Bible and think upon God's thoughts. Despite the distracting talk that is often going on around me, I use this block of time to prepare my heart for worship. (In fact, I believe if more members of the congregation devoted time to reading Scripture and praying for the service beforehand, church would be more meaningful for every worshiper.) Although the times and places where we meet God will vary, meeting alone with God each day should be a constant in our lives. After all, we are God's children, and like any good father, He wants to spend time with us.

"Okay," you say. "You've convinced me. I need to be more regular in my time with God—but exactly what should I do when I'm alone with Him?" I suggest that you read and meditate on God's Word for a while (devotional books like this one can help) and then spend some time in prayer. Talk to God as you would to your earthly parents or a special friend who loves you, desires the best for you, and wants to help you in every way possible. Here are a few suggestions:

- Praise God for who He is—the Creator and Sustainer of the universe who is interested in you, His child (Matthew 10:29-31).

- Thank God for all He has done for you, for all He is

doing for you, and for all that He will do for you in the
future (1 Thessalonians 5:18).

- Confess your sins. Tell God about those things you
  have done and said and thought for which you are sorry.
  Remember that He is "faithful and just and will forgive
  us our sins" whenever we confess them (1 John 1:9).

- Pray for your family. Pray for friends and neighbors who
  have needs—physical, emotional, or spiritual. Ask God
  to work in the heart of someone you hope will come to
  know Jesus as Savior. Pray for government officials, for
  your minister and church officers, and for missionaries
  and other Christian servants (Philippians 2:3-4).

- Pray for yourself. Ask for God's guidance in the day
  ahead. Ask Him to help you do His will and to arrange
  opportunities for you to serve Him throughout the day
  (Philippians 4:6).

Time with your heavenly Father is never wasted. If you spend
time alone with Him in the morning, you'll start your day refreshed
and ready for whatever comes your way. If you spend time alone
with Him in the evening, you'll go to sleep relaxed, resting in His
care, and wake up ready for a new day to serve Him.

Remember too that you can talk to Him anytime, anywhere—in
school, at work, on the freeway, at home—and about anything. You
don't have to make an appointment to ask Him for something you
need or to thank Him for something you've received from Him. God
is interested in everything that happens to you.

*Father God, thank You for the privilege of prayer—and for-
give me for taking it for granted. I want to spend time with
You each day. I want to know You better. I love You. Hear
my adoration, my confessions, my thanksgivings, and my*

supplications. Help me to live according to these desires despite all the demands I feel. And teach me, Lord, to call on You in every situation throughout the day. Thank You that You are always within the sound of my voice and always only a thought away. As I pray, help me be genuine with You, unconcerned about eloquence or impressive speech. Remind me to pause and listen to what You say to me. Amen.

Taking Action

- If you aren't already spending time with God each day, decide today that you will give it a try for one month.

- Tell someone of your commitment, and ask that person to hold you accountable.

- Read and pray Colossians 1:9-12 each day this month.

Reading On

Galatians 5:22-23	Galatians 3:26
John 1:12	Luke 5:16
Matthew 14:23	1 Peter 5:7

Lord, make me an
instrument of your peace.
Where there is hatred,
let me sow love;
where there is injury, pardon;
where there is doubt, faith;
where there is despair, hope;
where there is darkness, light;
and where there is sadness, joy.

O Divine Master,
grant that I may not
so much seek to be consoled
as to console;
to be understood
as to understand;
to be loved
as to love;
for it is in giving
that we receive;
it is in pardoning
that we are pardoned;
and it is in dying
that we are born to Eternal Life.

St. Francis of Assisi

God's Man for Life

SCRIPTURE READING: Job 1

KEY VERSE: Job 1:22
*In all this, Job did not sin by
charging God with wrongdoing.*

A landholder, rancher, and community leader, Job was one of the most respected and influential individuals in the entire region. Still, his number one priority was his large, active family. Despite the tremendous demands on him, he always had time for his children. They were never an interruption. And a person couldn't talk to him very long without him pulling from his wallet a favorite picture of his troop. He was always eager to tell you about each of them. This wise man knew that his most significant legacy wouldn't be his possessions or his bank accounts but his sons, daughters, and grandchildren. As a man living in the present but with a vision for the future, a man of God, a man whom God had greatly blessed, Job caught Satan's eye.

As the Lord holds court in the heavenlies, He asks Satan, "Have you considered my servant Job? There is no one on earth like him; he is blameless and upright, a man who fears God and shuns evil" (Job 1:8).

Satan shrugs and replies, in effect, "Of course Job is close with You. Who wouldn't be in his position? He's got all the advantages. You handle him softly and protect him. Just try taking away a few of his precious toys and then see what he does. He'll surely curse You to Your face" (verses 9-11).

For reasons unknown to us, God gives Satan some freedom to do what he wishes to test Job's faith. God does set limits, but even with those limits Satan causes Job to experience great loss and immeasurable pain. In a quick series of catastrophes, Job loses his business, his wealth, his health, and all 10 of his children. But still Job worships God. Then, with God's permission, Satan afflicts Job's body. At this point, Job's wife tells him to curse God and die (2:9). Would Job remain a man of God or would he reject the God who had once so richly blessed him? Is Job a man of character or a fair-weather follower of God?

Job remained God's man! By doing so, his life offers us many valuable lessons. One of these is the fact that things on the outside can be taken away from us, but no one can take away those things on the inside—our heart, our character, our soul. We can throw these away by turning from God and following after false gods, but no one can ever rob us of our heart and soul when we're committed to the Lord. And no one can take the character we develop as a result of our commitment.

So what will you do when the things of life are taken away from you? What will happen to your inner man? Will you stand strong in Christ? Will the loss purify and strengthen your character or will it break you?

We know that Job's trials strengthened his character, and people still talk about the patience of Job. But Job demonstrated more than these. He shows us a faith in God that has staying power and is able to endure to the end. As today's key verse says, "Through all [his losses and suffering] Job did not sin nor did he blame God" (Job 1:22 NASB).

And how does our faithful God respond to His people who have faith in Him? Read Job 42:10-16. May this passage give you hope when the circumstances of life bog you down. You can rejoice in the Lord in all situations and give thanks in whatever challenges that come your way because you know God is your faithful Redeemer.

Father God, thank You for all that You teach me through the life of Job. Thank You for showing me that my faith in You has staying power. May my life reflect the endurance of Job in whatever comes my way. Remind me to not measure my life by outward success; instead, help me see the internal as much more important. I want to make choices that preserve the character You're developing in me.

I pray that You, merciful God, will spare me from the kind of testing Job underwent. If I am to be tested, help me find strength in You. As I trust You with my life, increase my confidence that You know what I can handle and will not allow circumstances to overwhelm me. With You on my side, I can handle whatever comes my way. And when the trials are over, I know I will have grown even more into the person You want me to be. Amen.

Taking Action

■ List five commitments you've made in your life, and then answer the questions.

-
-
-
-
-

■ How are you doing with these commitments?

■ Which ones, if any, have fallen by the wayside? Why?

■ Are you satisfied with your progress? Why or why not?

■ Now list 5 blessings and thank God for each one of them.

-

-

-

-

-

■ Finally, list those areas of your life that are giving you difficulty. Thank God for each one because these struggles promote spiritual growth.

Reading On

This week read the rest of the book of Job. Reread this book whenever you feel you're being tested and need encouragement and hope.

What Your Kids Need to Hear

SCRIPTURE READING: Psalm 127

KEY VERSE: Psalm 127:3
*Children are a heritage from the LORD,
offspring a reward from him.*

Oh look, Daddy, I catched it!"

"That's my boy. Now get ready; here comes another. Make me proud and catch this one too."

"Look, Daddy, I'm only eight years old, and I can throw faster than anyone in the league!"

"But your batting stinks, Tiger. Can't play in the big leagues if you can't hit."

"Look, Dad, I'm 16, and I already made the varsity team."

"You better do a little less bragging and a little more practicing on your defense. Still need a lot of work."

"Look, Father, I'm 35, and the company has made me a vice president!"

"Maybe someday you'll start your own business like your old man. Then you'll really feel a sense of accomplishment."

"Look at me, Dad. I'm 40, successful, well-respected in the community. I have a wonderful wife and family—aren't you proud of me now, Dad?"

"All my life it seems I've caught everything but that one prize I wanted most—your approval. Can't you say it, Dad? Is it too much to ask for? Just once I'd like to know that feeling every child should have of being loved unconditionally. I'd like for you to put your arm around my shoulders and, instead of telling me I'm not good enough, tell me that in your eyes I'm already a winner and always will be no matter what."

"Look at me, Daddy. I'm all grown up…but in my heart still lives a little boy who yearns for his father's love. Won't you pitch me the words I've waited for all my life? I'll catch them, Father, I promise."[1]

Do your children know you love them? Do your kids know unconditional acceptance? Are your kids winners in your eyes—and do they know that? Our children need to know that Mom and Dad really love them. They long to hear us say, "I love you, and I am very proud of you." And they need to know of our love for them even when they…

- yell and scream in the grocery store
- have temper tantrums in the restaurant
- wear strange clothes
- have funny haircuts and oddly colored hair
- use vulgar language
- run away from home
- do poorly in school
- run around with friends we don't approve of

Often they are using behaviors like these to ask indirectly, "Do you love me?" What are they hearing from your reaction?

A good friend's son was not into sports like his dad desired. Instead, he was into motocross racing. When the parents went to see their pastor, the dad asked what he should do. The pastor said without hesitation (and not surprisingly), "Take up motocross!" Predictably, the dad said, "I don't like dirt, grease, motorcycles, the people who ride, sunburns, or the long days at the track." To this the pastor replied, "Fine—but how much do you love your son? Enough to get grease on your hands and clothes?" The following week our friend was off to the local motocross event with his son. They were soon very involved with dirt, grease, and people our friend would never have chosen to spend his weekends with. But through these actions, this father showed his son that he loved him.

Your children are a gift to you. The psalmist calls them "a heritage from the LORD…a reward from him" (Psalm 127:3). What are you doing to show your kids that you love them?

> *Father God, teach me to show my kids that I love them, and prompt me to tell them with words too. Help me be creative, unselfish, and willing to do things with them that aren't necessarily my first choice. Raising kids is a tough job, Lord. I need Your help. Amen.*

Taking Action

- Write each of your children—whatever their ages—a note to let them know how much you love them. Be specific about a few things you love about them.

- Spend some quality, one-on-one time with each of your children this week. Ask them what they want to do and then do it!

- On next month's calendar, schedule another date with each child.

Reading On

Psalm 127:3   Proverbs 16:24

Psalm 128:1-3   Proverbs 18:10

"I'm Too Busy Sawing"

SCRIPTURE READING: Exodus 20:8-11

KEY VERSES: Exodus 20:9-10

Six days you shall labor and do all your work,
but the seventh day is a sabbath to the LORD your God.
On it you shall not do any work...

⁘⁘

In *The Seven Habits of Highly Effective People,* author Steven R. Covey tells a story that reflects the need for rest, renewal, and reawakening in our lives.

> Suppose you come upon a man in the woods feverishly sawing down a tree.
>
> "You look exhausted!" you exclaim. "How long have you been at it?"
>
> "Over five hours," he replies, "and I'm beat. This is hard."
>
> "Maybe you could take a break for a few minutes and sharpen that saw. Then the work would go faster."
>
> "No time," the man says emphatically. "I'm too busy sawing."

To sharpen the saw means renewing ourselves in all four aspects of our natures:

> Physical—exercise, nutrition, stress management;
>
> Mental—reading, thinking, planning, writing;

Social/Emotional—service, empathy, security;

Spiritual—spiritual reading, study, and meditation.

To exercise in all these necessary dimensions, we must be proactive. No one can do it for us or make it urgent for us. We must do it for ourselves.[2]

Can you identify with the man sawing in the woods? I can. I know how hard it is to stop sawing even though I know that taking a break will help me come back stronger. And you may be a lot like me. But I've learned to take some breaks—and you can too.

In today's "Taking Action" section, you'll find some ideas for what to do when you stop sawing. Some of them may sound so good they'll help you put the saw down! When you do—when you take time to renew yourself—you'll be better equipped to handle the demands and stresses of life.

Like all of His commands, God's command to keep the Sabbath—to take time for rest—is for your own good. If you're tired, and weary, and maybe even fearful of what will happen if you put down the saw; if you're uptight, tense, and short-tempered, you're ready for renewal and reawakening. Take the risk and see what happens.

Father God, I'm often overwhelmed by all that needs to be done. It often feels like I just don't have time to stop sawing. Living a balanced life seems like an unreachable goal. Help me. Teach me moderation. Show me balance. Amen.

Taking Action

■ Here are a variety of suggestions for finding refreshment. Take a risk! Stop sawing, and see what it's like to live a life that's more in balance.

Physical

- Get a massage or take a sauna.
- Exercise regularly—walking, jogging, playing racquetball, swimming, and so forth.
- Read a book on nutrition and change to healthier eating habits.
- Take a stress-management class.
- Take a walk on a beach, by a lake, or along a mountain trail.
- Plant a garden.
- Walk or run in the rain.
- Volunteer for United Way, the Cancer Society, or the Heart Association.
- Help a friend in need.

Mental

- Listen to good music.
- Read a good magazine or book.
- Find a spot for meditating and reflecting.
- Spend some time alone.
- Write a letter to an old friend.
- Write out goals for the next three months.
- Enroll in a class at a local college.
- Think of possible changes to make in your life.
- List everything for which you're thankful.
- Learn to play an instrument.
- Memorize a favorite passage of Scripture.

Social/Emotional

- Have a good cry (yes, men cry).
- Have breakfast or lunch with a friend.
- Spend a day doing anything you want.
- Spend a quiet weekend with your wife just to regroup. Choose someplace close to avoid a long drive.
- Visit a friend.
- Make a new friend.
- Volunteer at a school, hospital, or church.
- Help a friend in need.

Spiritual

- Read the book of Psalms.
- Meditate on Scripture. Read a short passage and think long and hard about it.
- Read a book by a Christian author.
- Join a men's Bible study.
- Visit someone at the hospital or nursing home.
- Examine your motives (are you self-serving or serving others?).
- Listen to inspirational music.

■ Now add your own ideas to each of the four lists. Learn to take a break and take care of yourself. God knows the importance of rest. He gave us the Sabbath, and He calls us to be good stewards of the body, mind, and spirit He gave us. It's more than okay to take care of yourself—it's essential!

Reading On

Matthew 22:36-40   Exodus 20:2-18

Knowing God's Love

Scripture reading: 1 Corinthians 13:4-13

Key verses: 1 Corinthians 13:4-7

Love is patient, love is kind. It does not envy, it does not boast, it is not proud. It does not dishonor others, it is not self-seeking, it is not easily angered, it keeps no record of wrongs. Love does not delight in evil but rejoices with the truth. It always protects, always trusts, always hopes, always perseveres.

I vividly remember one momentous evening when Emilie and I were sitting on the couch in her mother's living room. I gently took Emilie's face in my hands and said, "Emilie, I love you, but I can't ask you to marry me." She was stunned. She couldn't understand why two people who were in love couldn't get married.

As I looked into her eyes, she asked, "Why not?" I answered firmly but gently, "Because you are not a Christian." Very innocently she asked me, "How do I become a Christian?" From that moment she began to consider whether Jesus might actually be the Messiah her Jewish people had long awaited.

After several months of seeking answers, Emilie prayed one evening at her bedside, "Dear God, if You have a Son, and if Your Son is Jesus our Messiah, please reveal Him to me!" She expected a voice to answer immediately, but God waited a few weeks to reveal Himself to her. Then, one Sunday morning, she responded to my pastor's challenge to accept Jesus Christ as her personal Savior. That evening she was baptized!

My being obedient to God has resulted in being blessed with a rich and wonderful marriage that is rooted in His love and dedicated to Him. Furthermore, vowing before God to love Emilie through the good times and the bad reinforced my commitment to Him when the times were indeed bad. Had my vows been to Emilie alone, I might have walked away. But God's witness of our vows and the foundation He gives to Christian couples enables us to stand together whatever comes our way.

My friend, God loves us even though we're far from perfect. At those times when we're very much aware of our failings, we need to remember that we have value because we are God's. And knowing of God's love for us empowers us to better love other people. God's unconditional love inspires us to demonstrate the characteristics of love the apostle Paul described to the Christians in Corinth. Today read 1 Corinthians 13 as a reminder of the strength and attributes of love God's way.

You've probably seen this bumper sticker: "Please be patient with me. God isn't finished with me yet." God is still working in our lives, and He'll never give up on us. As you become more confident of God's love for you, you'll find that people's opinions and judgments don't matter as much. Assured of God's unfailing love, you'll want to serve Him and Him alone in full obedience.

> *Father God, help me confidently share Your love in words and actions with others so they might come to know You. I want to honor my commitment to You by standing strong in my faith in You and remaining obedient and steadfast. May others see You and the characteristics of Your love in me. Please give me opportunities to encourage others because they too are works in progress! Amen.*

Taking Action

- What evidence do you have that God loves you? Make a list and then thank Him for these blessings.

■ When has God used your obedience to bless you, another
person, or a situation?

■ Put your love into action. What can you do for your wife
or significant other? How can you get involved at church?
Can you help the homeless in some way this week? Could a
local mission use your talents or capabilities for a few hours
this weekend? What handyman projects could you do for
an elderly neighbor?

Reading On

Matthew 5:46   1 John 4:12

The Call to Unity

Scripture reading: Genesis 2:20-25

Key verse: Genesis 2:24 nasb
*For this reason a man shall leave his father and
his mother, and be joined to his wife;
and they shall become one flesh.*

One of Aesop's fables is the story of a wise father who, noticing disharmony among his sons, called them together to discuss the strife. He told each of his four sons to bring a twig to the meeting. As the young men assembled, the father took each boy's twig and easily snapped it in half. Then he gathered four twigs, tied them together in a bundle, and asked each son to break the bundle. Each one tried but to no avail. The bundle would not snap.

After the sons had tried valiantly to break the bundle, the father asked his boys what they learned from the exercise. The eldest son spoke up. "If we are individuals, anyone can break us, but if we stick together, no one can harm us." The father said, "You're right! You must always stand together to be strong."

What is true for the four brothers is equally true for a husband and wife. If we don't stand together and let God make us one in spite of our differences, we will easily be defeated. That is one reason why, in today's passage, God calls a husband and wife to...

- departure ("a man will leave his father and mother")
- permanence ("and be united to his wife")
- oneness ("and they will become one flesh")

Together, these three elements help make a marriage strong. Now let's consider oneness. In God's sight, we become one at the altar when we say our vows to one another and before Him. But in reality, oneness is a *process* that happens over a period of time, over a lifetime together.

And becoming one with another person can be a very difficult process. It isn't easy to change from being independent and self-centered to sharing every aspect of your life and self with another person. The difficulty is often intensified when we marry later in life and are more set in our ways or, as was the case for Emilie and me, when you and your spouse come from very different religious views or financial backgrounds. Emilie, for instance, came from a family headed by an alcoholic father, and she suffered from a verbally and physically abusive father. I came from a warm, loving family where yelling and screaming simply didn't happen.

Although it took Emilie and me only a few minutes to say our vows and enter into oneness in God's eyes, we've spent more than 50 years blending our lives and building the oneness which we enjoy today. Becoming one doesn't mean becoming the same, however. Oneness means sharing the same degrees of commitment to the Lord and to the marriage, the same goals and dreams, and the same mission in life. Oneness is an internal conformity to each other, not external conformity. It doesn't look like the Marines, with their short haircuts, shiny shoes, straight backs, and military bearing. The oneness and internal conformity of a marriage relationship comes through the unselfish act of allowing God to shape us into the marriage partners He would have us be. Oneness results when two individuals reflect Christ. Such spiritual oneness produces tremendous strength and unity in a marriage and family.

For this oneness to happen, the two marriage partners must leave their families and let God make them one. We husbands help the cleaving happen when we show—not just tell—our wives that they are our most important priority after God. Likewise, our wives need to let us know how important we are to them. We husbands don't need to be competing with our wives' fathers or any other males for the number one position in their lives. You and I must know that our wives respect, honor, and love us to help us fulfill our roles as husbands. And our clear communication of our love for our wives will strengthen the bond of marriage and encourage them to love and respect us.

Now consider the words Paul writes to the church at Philippi: "Make my joy complete by being of the same mind, maintaining the same love, united in spirit, intent on one purpose" (Philippians 2:2 NASB). This verse has guided me as I've worked to unite my family in purpose, thought, and deed. After many years of working at it, I can say that we're truly united in our purpose and direction. If you were to ask Emilie to state our goals, her answers would match mine: "Seek first [your heavenly Father's] kingdom and his righteousness, and all these things will be given to you." As we face decisions, we need to ask ourselves, "Are we seeking God's kingdom and His righteousness? Will doing this help His kingdom come and help us experience His righteousness? Or are we seeking our own edification or our own satisfaction?" These questions guide Emilie and me when we have to make a decision on an issue, and that oneness of purpose helps make our marriage work.

God calls us to permanence and oneness in a marriage, qualities the world neither values nor encourages. Knowing what God intends marriage to be and working to leave, cleave, and become one with our spouses will help us shine His light in a very dark world.

Father God, today's reading has helped me realize that there are several areas in my marriage where my wife and I need to be more united. Show me how to help work toward unity in purpose and spirit. I thank You now for what You are going to do in our marriage. Amen.

Taking Action

▪ Set a date with your wife and, when you're together, write down five things you agree on regarding family, discipline, manners, values, home, church, and so forth.

▪ Now list any issues you don't yet agree on. State the differences and discuss them. Agree to pray about them, and set a time to discuss these items again.

▪ Say, "I love you" in a way you don't usually say it.

  • Fill a heart-shaped box with jelly beans, chocolates, or jewelry.

  • Give a certificate for a massage, a facial, or a weekend getaway.

  • Have firewood delivered—and then use it!

▪ We husbands show we care when we pay attention to small details.

  • Instead of handing her a pack of gum, unwrap a piece for her.

  • Pull out her chair as she sits down for a meal, whether at home or dining out.

  • Open the car door for her. Help her get in and out of the car.

  • Place a flower on her pillow.

Reading On

Philippians 2:2   Matthew 19:3-6

Matthew 6:33   1 Corinthians 6:19-20

Rejected by Men

SCRIPTURE READING: Isaiah 53:3-12

KEY VERSE: Isaiah 53:3
*He was despised and rejected by mankind, a man
of suffering, and familiar with pain.*

We've all experienced the pain of rejection, perhaps even by someone we care about very deeply—a parent, wife, child, brother, sister, friend, or possibly all of them. Jesus experienced rejection too. If anyone knows the pain it causes, He does. His own people whom He came to save were the very ones who nailed Him to a cross. As the apostle John said, "He came to that which was his own, but his own did not receive him" (John 1:11).

My wife, Emilie, knows rejection from her people too. Her Jewish family wanted her to marry within their faith. Yet when she was 16, I introduced her to Christ. Within a few months of her accepting Him as Savior, we were engaged. Eight months later we were married. Some of Emilie's family members rejected her because of her stand for Jesus and her decision to marry me, a Christian man.

God has honored Emilie's faithfulness to Him, and her family has come to respect and love me. Family unity has been restored, although it didn't happen overnight. In God's time, one by one, hearts were softened and attitudes changed. Emilie hung in there and loved her family when it was difficult because of their attitudes toward us and their mockery of our Christian faith. She's grateful today that she trusted Jesus.

Emilie was rejected because she trusted the Savior whom Isaiah prophesied would be despised and rejected by mankind. Jesus' fore-knowledge of what was to come, however, didn't make His experi-ence any less painful. At least Emilie could turn to God in her pain. Jesus felt rejected momentarily by His Father. As Jesus bore the sins of the world, He cried out, "My God, my God, why have you for-saken me?" (Matthew 27:46).

Despite all this rejection, Jesus never abandoned the mission God assigned Him. He never fought back against the ones who rejected Him. Instead, Jesus responded with love—even for those who nailed Him to the cross.

When you're feeling rejected, remember that the Lord knows how you feel and that He offers you His strength to get through it. The Bible says that Jesus sympathizes with our weaknesses and offers His grace for our times of need. When Jesus suffered on the cross, He bore our penalty. He paid the price for our sins. God gave us this promise: "Never will I leave you; never will I forsake you" (Hebrews 13:5).

No matter what happens, know that God will never reject you. You will never be alone again. You may be rejected by others, but God Almighty will always be here to comfort you.

Father God, You know how I needed to be reminded of this truth from Scripture today. You know the rejection I've expe-rienced at work, in my family, by friends. I lay before You all these hurts and ask for Your comfort and peace. Thank You for Your promise that You will always be near me. I need You today. Amen.

Taking Action

- Write down what rejections—recent or distant—still cause you pain.

- Rather than dwell on your pain, place it in Jesus' hands today using a prayer based on 1 Peter 5:7. Start with something like, "Lord, I cast my cares upon You because I know You care for me."

■ Despite the pain you're feeling, spend some time today thanking God that He will never forsake you and that, even if your mother, father, sister, brother, or friend forsake you, He will take care of you (Deuteronomy 4:31; Psalm 27:10).

Reading On

John 1:2	Hebrews 4:15-16
Hebrews 13:5	2 Corinthians 1:3-7
Philippians 4:13	

The Minimum
Daily Requirement

SCRIPTURE READING: Ephesians 2:4-9

KEY VERSES: Ephesians 2:8-9
*It is by grace you have been saved, through faith—
and this not from yourselves, it is the gift of God—
not by works, so that no one can boast.*

Several years ago a young college student asked me, "As a Christian, how much beer can I drink?" Others questions I've been asked include:

- How long should I read my Bible each day?
- How long should I pray each day?
- How much money do I have to give to the church?
- Do I have to sing in the choir to be a good Christian?
- How many times a week must I be in church?

It's like some people want to know what the "minimum daily requirement" is for being a Christian. What do we really have to do day-by-day to get by? After all, we're interested in daily nutritional requirements when it comes to our food. Shouldn't we be as concerned when it comes to our Christian walk and our spiritual health? Of course! It only makes sense that we would want to know how long we should pray, how long we should read the Bible, how much money we should put in in the offering plate, how many church activities we should participate in each week, and so forth.

Paul addresses these very basic concerns in his letter to the Christians in Ephesus. He very clearly states, "It is by grace you have been saved, through faith—and this not from yourselves, it is the gift of God—not by works, so that no one can boast" (Ephesians 2:8-9). Put differently, Christ has freed us from bondage to minimum daily requirements. Our relationship with the Lord Jesus is not contingent on works; instead, it is a gift of grace.

"So," you ask, "do I do nothing as a Christian? Aren't there any requirements?" The Scriptures challenge us to be like Christ, and if we are to do that, we need to open the Bible and learn how Jesus loved and lived. When we do so, we see that Jesus

- studied God's Word
- spent time with believers (and non-believers)
- prayed regularly
- served those around Him who were in need

Christ didn't do these things because He was told to do them. He did them because He *wanted* to. He did them out of love.

So what is your minimum daily requirement when it comes to your spiritual health? It will be determined by love. So let your loving God guide you as you go through your day. Let your love for Him shape your Bible study, prayer time, giving, and other involvements. Your walk will look different from everyone else's, and that's okay as long as you're sure you're doing what God wants you to do.

Father God, help me not worry about "how long" or "how often" as I work toward living a life that pleases You. Put a strong desire in my soul to spend time with You today in prayer and study, not so I am doing what I should, but because I love You and want to know You better. In those quiet moments, let time stand still so I can forget about my schedule, commitments, and pressures as I worship You. Amen.

Taking Action

- List the things you're doing because you should, because you think they are required of you as a Christian. Now cross off those items you're doing joylessly and out of a sense of compulsion.

- Why are you still doing those things left on your list? Cross out any other items you're doing because you should rather than because you love God.

- Now list only those activities you *want* to do because you love the Lord and want to be more like Christ. This may be similar to your previous list, but now the items are ones you want to do. Simply stated, you're learning to live in grace and not under law.

Reading On

1 Corinthians 1:4-8	Ephesians 6:10
2 Timothy 1:9-10	James 4:6
2 Corinthians 12:9	

A New Heart

Scripture reading: Ezekiel 36:24-27

Key verse: Ezekiel 36:26

I will give you a new heart and put a new spirit in you.

As you spend time with God regularly, you'll realize that you, with your old heart, can't do what is necessary to make yourself a godly person. In fact, none of us can make that transformation happen under our own power. Fortunately we don't have to according to today's key verse! God offers us a heart transplant—one that is even more remarkable than the transplants doctors do today.

Thankfully, most of us will not need a new physical heart, but we all need a new spiritual heart. Why? Because we're born with a sinful nature. God lets us know that through David's writing: "Behold, I was brought forth in iniquity, and in sin my mother conceived me" (Psalm 51:5 NASB). The prophet Jeremiah wrote: "The heart is deceitful above all things and beyond cure" (Jeremiah 17:9). Jesus taught the same lesson: "Out of the heart come evil thoughts, murders, adulteries, fornications, thefts, false witness, slanders" (Matthew 15:19 NASB). The apostle Paul wrestled with his sin nature: "The good that I want, I do not do, but I practice the very evil that I do not want. But if I am doing the very thing I do not want, I am no longer the one doing it, but sin which dwells in me" (Romans 7:19-20 NASB). And the apostle John is very direct in his statement about sin: "If we say that we have no sin, we are deceiving ourselves and the truth is not in us" (1 John 1:8 NASB).

So what are we to do? Not even the most skilled physician can cure a sinful heart or give us a new, pure one. But God can! And according to His promises, He will. In *Seeing Yourself Through God's Eyes*, June Hunt talks about this process:

> Slowly, after this divine transplant, healing begins and, as promised, your new heart becomes capable of perfect love. Your self-centeredness is now Christ-centeredness. There is healing to replace the hatred; there is a balm for the bitterness. You can face the world with a freedom and a future you have never known before.
>
> "Create in me a clean heart, O God, and renew a stead-fast spirit within me" (Psalm 51:10). Once you have a changed heart, you have a changed life. You can love the unlovable, be kind to the unkind, and forgive the unfor-givable. All this because you have a new heart—you have God's heart![3]

This kind of heart operation performed by the loving hands of your divine Physician doesn't require major medical insurance. There are no disclaimers or deductibles. God offers this transforma-tion to us free of charge. It cost Him greatly—He gave His only Son for our salvation—but it's a gift to us. All we have to do is accept it—no strings attached.

Father God, You know that I need a new heart—not one that a doctor transplants but one touched, healed, and changed by You. I want that new heart with new desires, new direction, and new purpose, all of which honor and glorify You. Thank You for all that You're going to do in my life. Amen.

Taking Action

- List five areas in your life where you see the need for a new heart, for God's heart.

-
-
-
-
-

■ Now, for each item you listed, write down two or three activities you can do to be God's man in each situation. Know that God alone can change your heart, but you can make choices to work with Him in the process.

■ Talk to a friend who will pray for you, encourage you, and hold you accountable in these areas.

Reading On

Psalm 51:5   Romans 7:19-20

Matthew 15:19   1 John 1:8

Romans 5:5

"Create in me a pure heart, O God,
and renew a steadfast spirit within me."

Psalm 51:10

God Will Provide

SCRIPTURE READING: Genesis 22:7-8

KEY VERSES: Genesis 22:7-8

"The fire and wood are here," Isaac said,
"but where is the lamb for the burnt offering?"

Abraham answered, "God himself will provide
the lamb for the burnt offering, my son."
And the two of them went on together.

Emilie and I were firm about teaching our children these words as they were growing up. "Come" and "stop" helped us raise our children because children who learn them learn obedience. As God's children, these are words we need to listen for so we can willingly obey Him.

Abraham is a striking example of obedience to God even when God puts Abraham to the ultimate test. God instructed Abraham to take his son Isaac to the region of Moriah and sacrifice him there as a burnt offering. What must Abraham have thought? He deeply loved Isaac, the miracle child for whom he and his wife, Sarah, had prayed long and hard. And now God was asking him to kill him.

Early the next morning, Abraham, Isaac, and two servants got ready to leave. Having cut enough wood for the burnt offering, they set out as God had instructed. "On the third day Abraham looked up and saw the place in the distance. He said to his servants, 'Stay here with the donkey while I and the boy go over there. *We* will worship and then *we* will come back to you'" (Genesis 22:5).

Did you catch that? Abraham said, "*We* will worship...*we* will come back." Abraham, who had experienced the mighty power of God when he received the gift of his son late in his life, trusted God and kept moving ahead in obedience to Him. I'm sure the servants were puzzled, as was Isaac. Where was the animal for the sacrifice? The servants didn't ask, and Isaac didn't ask until later.

"Abraham took the wood for the burnt offering and placed it on his son Isaac, and he himself carried the fire and the knife" (verse 6). Perhaps in his early teens or maybe a little younger, Isaac was old enough to carry the heavy wood.

As they walked to the place God told him, Abraham and Isaac talked.

"Isaac spoke up and said to his father Abraham, 'Father?' 'Yes, my son?' Abraham replied. 'The fire and the wood are here,' Isaac said, 'but where is the lamb for the burnt offering?'" (verse 7). Where would they find a lamb in the wilderness?

Hear Abraham's reply! "God himself will provide the lamb for the burnt offering, my son" (verse 8).

So the two of them went on together until they reached the place God had indicated. Once there, Abraham removed the wood from Isaac's back, built an altar for worship, and then arranged the wood on top. He bound his son and placed him on top of the wood. The Bible doesn't reveal anything about Isaac's words or thoughts. Perhaps because of Abraham's trust and belief, Isaac knew too that God would provide. And maybe he was willing to die for God. Whatever Isaac was thinking or feeling, there he was, bound and lying on top of the wood he himself had carried.

Everything was in place. It was time for the sacrifice. "[Abraham] reached out his hand and took the knife to slay his son" (verse 10). Abraham's arm was lifted up, ready to plunge the knife into Isaac, when "the angel of the Lord called out to him from heaven, 'Abraham! Abraham!'" (verse 11). Abraham immediately stopped. The angel continued, "'Do not lay a hand on the boy,' he said. 'Do not do anything to him. Now I know that you fear God, because you have not withheld from me your son, your only son.' Abraham looked up and there in a thicket he saw a ram caught by its horns. He went and took the ram and sacrificed it as a burnt offering instead of his son." That was a close call!

Abraham named that place on the mountain "The Lord Will Provide" (verse 14). He hadn't doubted that God would provide. Can you imagine what the two servants must have thought when they saw Abraham and Isaac return without firewood but with a bloodstained knife? Did Abraham tell them how God had provided a ram for the offering?

Abraham obeyed when God told him to prepare to sacrifice his son. And, when the angel called his name, Abraham stopped to listen. Had Abraham not obeyed, he and Isaac wouldn't have seen God provide for them so graciously. With obedience came a greater knowledge of God and His mercy and love.

How does your level of obedience compare with Abraham's? It's easy to say we trust God, but then we often go ahead and take the situation into our own hands, trying to move ahead in our power and not allowing the Lord to provide. When we do so, we miss out on experiencing God's faithfulness.

What do you need to trust God for today? Where do you need Him to provide for you? God is calling you to come to His altar so that you can watch Him provide. So despite the pressures of the day, stop and worship Him. During those quiet moments, tell God about your concerns and let Him remind you that He will provide.

Father God, I will obey when I hear Your voice and stop when You say to. Give me ears to hear You and a heart to respond quickly. When I worship, teach me what You want me to know. Remind me of Your faithfulness as I trust You for the present and the future. Thank You for providing everything I need. Amen.

Taking Action

- Choose a place in your home where you can worship—and then use it.

- How will you worship God there?

- What will stopping and listening to Him look like?

- What will you tell God that reveals how much you trust Him?

- Will you praise Him for providing everything you need through prayer, or song, or both?

- Purpose to obey His Word throughout the week.

Reading On

Galatians 4:28   Hebrews 11:17-19

A Five-Cent Cone

SCRIPTURE READING: Proverbs 4:1-9

KEY VERSE: Proverbs 4:7 (NASB)

With all your acquiring, get understanding.

Actor Kirk Douglas wrote his autobiography and called it *The Son of the Ragman*. In it, he talks about his growing-up years with parents who had recently emigrated from Russia. He recalls that his mother was warm and supportive as she did her best to adjust to a new country, but he remembers his father as stern, untrusting, strict, and cold. Unaccustomed to giving words of encouragement, a pat on the back, or a hug, his father remained a distant and very private man. But then Douglas shares this story about his father.

One evening at school, the young Kirk Douglas had a major role speaking, dancing, and singing in a play. He knew his mother would be there, but he seriously doubted that his father would go. To his amazement and surprise, about halfway through the program he caught sight of his father standing in the back of the auditorium.

After completing the evening's program, he wanted his father to come up and congratulate him for a job well done, but true to fashion, his father wasn't able to say much. Instead, he asked his son if he'd like to stop and get a five-cent ice cream cone. As Kirk Douglas reflects back over all the awards he's received, he prizes that five-cent ice cream cone the most—even more than his Oscar.

As fathers, we don't always realize the important role we play in family life. Our children hunger for our approval. They want and need to know beyond a shadow of a doubt that we love them and care about what's going on in their lives. Our kids need our words, but they also need our presence. They need us to spend time with them. And sometimes giving of our time says what we can't seem to say out loud.

In today's key verse, God calls us to acquire understanding. I challenge you to work on understanding your children better. Don't assume you already know what they're thinking and feeling. Let them tell you and then be ready to laugh when they laugh and cry when they cry. Be a dad they know really cares about the small and the big events in their lives.

> *Father God, today help me be an encourager to my children. You know how hard that is for me. Teach me to speak approving words and show them unconditional acceptance. I want to be a father who understands his kids. Help me start today. Amen.*

Taking Action

- Take your kids out for ice cream. Make these dates special occasions for them. Let each of them know they are important to you.

- Sometime today take your children aside one at a time, give them hugs, and tell them you truly love them.

Reading On

Proverbs 2:6-7   Proverbs 1:7

Not on Your Permanent Record

SCRIPTURE READING: Romans 8:1-9

KEY VERSES: Romans 8:1-2

*There is now no condemnation for those who
are in Christ Jesus, because through Christ Jesus the
law of the Spirit who gives life has set you free
from the law of sin and death.*

An incident from the boyhood days of Dr. Craig Merrihew vividly illustrates the great promise in today's Scripture passage. When Craig was in the fifth grade, he and a friend rode their bicycles to school each day. School started at 9:00 A.M., and they weren't allowed on the playground before 8:30. One day the tailwinds were in their favor, and the boys arrived at the playground early. The fact that there was no supervision didn't stop them, and they were having a great time when a teacher finally arrived and sent the boys directly to the principal's office.

When they got to Mr. Fox's office, the two had to sit and wait, all the while wondering what was going to happen to them. Would they get detention? Would they be expelled? Would the principal call the police? Would Mr. Fox call their parents to come get them? Their knees and their voices were shaking by the time Mr. Fox appeared and invited the boys into his office.

After hearing the story, Mr. Fox stood up and said authoritatively, "This will go on your permanent record"—the worst sentence Craig thought he could receive. He just knew this would keep him from graduating from elementary school, junior high school, high school, college, medical school, and definitely keep him from becoming a dentist. He also knew that his parents would be very upset.

When Craig got home that evening, he told his dad what had happened. His dad assured Craig that this event wouldn't get in the way of any graduation ceremony or career plans. What words and assurance of freedom! Craig wouldn't be condemned forever because of an early arrival on the school playground.

Have you ever been discouraged because you, like Craig, thought that some sin was on your "permanent record"? The apostle Paul assures us that "there is now no condemnation for those who are in Christ Jesus." We are never to forget that, at one time, we were the focus of God's holy and just wrath. But neither are we to forget that Christ Jesus came into the world to save sinners—to save you and me. Being aware of our sinfulness makes us even more appreciative of the fact that Jesus died on the cross in our place to pay for our sins and wipe our slates clean. Jesus, the sinless One, bore our sins and endured the wrath of God for us. When we view the cross at Calvary from this perspective, we see the love of God.

In fact, the love of God has no meaning apart from what happened at Calvary, and Calvary has no meaning apart from the holy and just wrath of God. Jesus didn't die just to give us peace and purpose in life; He died to save us from the wrath of God. He died to reconcile us to our holy God from whom we were alienated because of our sin. Jesus died to ransom us from the penalties of sin—everlasting destruction and being cut off from the presence of God. Jesus died so that we—the sinners who deserve God's wrath—can become through grace God's children and heirs. Put simply, Jesus died so that our sins wouldn't be on our permanent records.

For reassurance that your sins—past, present, and future—are forgiven because of Jesus' death on the cross, heed these words written for you: "If we confess our sins, [God] is faithful and just and will forgive us our sins and purify us from all unrighteousness" (1 John 1:9).

God's Word offers you total assurance that your sins will not be on your permanent record when you stand before God on judgment day.

Father God, thank You for sending Your Son to pay for my sins. Thank You for the reassurance that all of my sins—past, present, and future—have been wiped off my permanent record because of Jesus' death and resurrection. Amen.

Taking Action

■ Spend some time today in private confession. Ask God to forgive you and purify you.

■ Record this date and mark 1 John 1:9 in your Bible so when you look back you will be reminded that God forgives you.

Reading On

1 John 1:9	Luke 18:9-14
Matthew 5:1-10	Romans 5:14-17

Marriage Preservation

SCRIPTURE READING: Proverbs 17:14-22

KEY VERSE: Proverbs 17:17
*A friend loves at all times, and
a brother is born for a time of adversity.*

Ed and Carol Neuenschwander (a pastor and his wife) shared this in their book *Two Friends in Love*:

> Although the shell of a union may endure, the spirit of the marriage may disintegrate in time unless mates take periodic and shared reprieves from the pressures they live under.
>
> The pressures we must often escape are not those we create for ourselves, but those brought into our lives from the outside. Nonetheless, they can wear our relationships thin.
>
> The key to keeping a cherished friendship alive may be found in breaking away long enough and frequently enough to keep ourselves fresh and our love growing. And usually that involves childless weekends. Without such moments of focused attention, it's difficult to keep the kind of updated knowledge of one another that keeps two hearts in close proximity alive and growing together. A growing marriage needs refreshed inhabitants.[4]

We live in a very hectic world that cries out for stillness, quietness, and aloneness. For the sake of our marriages and our mental health, we must seek solitude as couples. Such quiet times for regrouping won't just happen. We must plan for these special times with our mates.

Throughout our years together, Emilie and I have made it a point to get away from the noise and busyness of life and be by ourselves. We don't set a schedule. We sleep in and disregard clocks. We eat when and if we want to. We spend time—quality and quantity—together. I encourage you to find a time when you and your wife can do the same. Our favorite time for these getaways has been in late December and early January. Whenever you go, be sure to get away from everything not related to your love relationship with your wife. Set aside time to write out some personal and family goals. With each goal, include some specific action steps and a rough timetable. Slow down and consider your life together.

When was the last time you had extended time alone as a couple? You may be thinking, *It's been a while, but we don't have the money to get away!* Don't let excuses keep you from doing what you need to do to preserve your marriage. I've found that we human beings usually manage to do what we really want to do. You'll find ways to save money for time away if your marriage truly is a top priority.

> *Father God, I want the strongest, most satisfying marriage possible. Give me wisdom as I speak to my wife about scheduling a time out for the two of us. Help us follow through and strengthen our commitment to each other. Teach me to slow down to be alone with You…and with my wife. Amen.*

Taking Action

- Plan a special day for you and your wife. Get away for at least one night (two or three if you can).

- Set aside funds for this adventure.

- Mail your wife a special letter of invitation.

- Keep your expectations for this time modest. Too many expectations lead to disappointments. Take off the pressure. Let this time with your wife be relaxed and stress free.

- Aside from this special overnighter, what will you do to know your wife better? Express your appreciation? Communicate better? Listen more? Share what you're feeling? Romance her? Write your ideas down and then choose several to accomplish this month.

- How can you remind yourself to take the time just to hold her? To be affectionate?

Reading On

1 Corinthians 13:3-8

Dealing with Rejection

Scripture reading: John 3:16-21

Key verse: John 3:16
*God so loved the world that he gave
his one and only Son, that whoever believes in him
shall not perish but have eternal life.*

When have you experienced rejection? Did it come with that gal in high school, a marriage proposal, college entrance applications, missed promotions, a home loan you didn't qualify for? Now think about how you reacted to the rejection. Did you feel hurt? Angry? Both? Whom did you go to for advice?

When we experience rejection, we can go to Jesus for comfort and guidance. He understands what we're going through. He who was nailed to the cross knows about rejection. Isaiah prophesied that Jesus would be despised and rejected by mankind (Isaiah 53:3). The people He came to save were the very ones who had Him nailed to that wooden instrument of death (John 1:10-11). On the cross, Jesus shouted to God in heaven, "My God, my God, why have you forsaken me?" (Matthew 27:46). Even Jesus felt rejected and alone. Despite the rejection He encountered, Jesus...

- never abandoned the mission God had given to Him
- never retaliated against those who scorned Him
- responded in love

According to the writer of the book of Hebrews, Jesus sympathizes with our weakness and pain and gives us His grace to help us when we're hurting. These promises written so many years ago are for you and me today too:

- "Never will I leave you; never will I forsake you" (Hebrews 13:5).

- "Praise be to the God…who comforts us in all our troubles, so that we can comfort those in any trouble with the comfort we ourselves receive from God" (2 Corinthians 1:3-4).

- "You also were included in Christ when you heard the message of truth, the gospel of your salvation. When you believed, you were marked in him with a seal, the promised Holy Spirit" (Ephesians 1:13).

Jesus is with us when we're rejected. He will comfort us, and the Holy Spirit will give us peace. When we're rejected, we can choose to let bitterness, depression, anger, fear, doubt, and loneliness dominate our lives. But these negative emotions can destroy us; they can give Satan a foothold in our lives. Or, when we feel rejected, we can go to our God the Redeemer. He will comfort us and then give us the strength to "forgive, to love our enemies, and to pray for those who persecute us" (Matthew 5:44). Those commands are for our good. Obeying them frees us from the bitterness that kills our spirit and blocks our relationship with God. And it's only when we adopt Christ's attitude of forgiveness that we experience fully His healing.

When you respond to rejection with God's love, people will notice. They'll be drawn to Christ, God will be glorified, and you will experience freedom from the past and from the pain you felt. Forgiveness isn't easy, but it's what God calls us to do. It's what Jesus—who knows rejection—helps us do.

Jesus, You know what rejection feels like, and I do too. When those times come, remind me to turn to You. And when I think about rejections in the past, help me trust in Your steadfast love for me, Your perfect plan for my life, and Your power to redeem the negative. With Your guidance and strength, I will forgive where and when I need to. And when I am tempted to reject someone, encourage me to extend Your love instead. Amen.

Taking Action

- Make a list of the times you've experienced some kind of rejection. What has God taught you from those times? How has He used those times to develop your Christian character?

- If some of the events you listed still cause pain, talk to God about it. Ask Him what He would have you do, if anything. Be willing to take the step if He seems to be directing you to make a visit, pick up the phone, or write a letter.

- Turn to the Bible for assurances of God's unshakable and eternal love for you despite how someone may be treating you.

Reading On

Philippians 4:13

When Mamma Ain't Happy,
Ain't Nobody Happy

SCRIPTURE READING: Proverbs 24

KEY VERSES: Proverbs 24:3-4

*By wisdom a house is built, and through understanding
it is established; through knowledge its rooms are
filled with rare and beautiful treasures.*

When Emilie and I were shopping in the Marketplace in Charleston, South Carolina, a booth displaying handmade dolls caught our attention. I noticed right away the one whose apron bore the words, "When Mamma ain't happy, ain't nobody happy." I smiled to myself and showed Emilie the doll. Smiling as well, she said, "So true! If Mom's happy, the whole family is happy."

But you probably already knew that. As husbands, we can help make the whole family happy if we make sure Mamma is happy! If we spend time knowing our wives and finding out what makes them tick—and ticked—we will truly enrich our family's lives.

I'm not saying that we're responsible for another person's happiness, because we aren't. Each one of us is responsible to find our own happiness. However, we husbands can set the stage for our wives so that their happiness can flourish. And when that happens, we will receive riches and blessings in return. Women give their all to their families when they feel appreciated and when they know their husbands care about their thoughts, their feelings, and their daily world.

So think about it for a minute. How well do you know your

wife? What are you doing to keep her happy—to meet her needs and to let her know you love and appreciate her? Are you spending the time with her she needs? Are you listening when she wants to talk? Start today to do these things, and you'll be empowering her to be a more loving mother and wife. And when Mamma's happy, everybody's happy!

Father God, forgive me for taking for granted the blessing of my wife. Show me where I've been insensitive and unappreciative. Help me every day to let her know how much I love her and how much I appreciate all she does for our family. I want her to realize that I see Christ reflected in her life. I truly want her to know that she is a blessing to me. Amen.

Taking Action

- Surprise your wife with an impromptu date. Call her and say, "Get dressed up. I'm taking you somewhere special for dinner tonight." Choose a romantic setting. Be sure to line up a babysitter if you need one. Don't leave that to her.

- Leave your wife a small present—a single flower, a piece of her favorite candy, a small stuffed animal somewhere in the house where she'll find it. Don't forget a card that tells her how much you appreciate her.

Reading On

Proverbs 9:1-6   Proverbs 16:1-4

Proverbs 4:5

In His Steps

Scripture reading: 1 Peter 2:13-25

Key verse: 1 Peter 2:21

To this you were called, because Christ suffered
for you, leaving you an example, that you
should follow in his steps.

Many years ago I read Charles M. Sheldon's book *In His Steps,* the story of a man who made a conscious effort to walk in the steps of Jesus. Before saying anything, doing anything, going anywhere, or making any decisions, he asked himself what Jesus would do and then he tried to do the same. Although living like Jesus was nearly impossible, this experience changed the man's life forever.

During our time on earth, daily situations will reveal our character—but will our character point others toward Jesus? We do well to look to Jesus and His example of a godly life. He showed us how to live with kindness, gentleness, sympathy, and affection. He was always loving, forgiving, merciful, and patient. He had a sense of justice and compassion for the suffering and persecuted, and He willingly took a stand for what was right in God's eyes. We can learn much from Him.

God also tells us through His Word that Jesus knows our pain, our grief, and the tragedy of friends who betray. He knows how hard it is to live in a world full of sickness and sin that we can do very little about. What we *can* do—and this is following in Jesus' footsteps—is bring people to Him, to the One who forgives, heals, and helps. We can also let God work in our hearts and lives so that

He can make us more Christlike. No, we can't be exactly like Jesus. Our humanness and sin get in the way. But we can develop a teachable spirit. We can love God with all our hearts, souls, minds, and strength. We can let Him transform us into more selfless and more joyful people so that our character will more accurately reveal the likeness of Jesus.

As Jesus' representatives in the world today, we walk in His steps when we follow His call to us—when we help the helpless, pray for the sick, feed and clothe the homeless, and support those whom God lifts up to be missionaries. Let's walk in Jesus' footsteps today and respond willingly to His call to serve.

> *Father God, You know I want to be more like Your Son, Jesus, and I long for the wisdom only You can give. Grant me today some new revelation, and help me step out and trust You in a new way. May the time I spend meditating on Your Word and talking to You help me know You even better. Help that awareness make me more able and willing to walk in Your steps. Amen.*

Taking Action

- How teachable are you? What can you do to be more open to what God wants you to learn?

- What will you do to follow in Jesus' steps today?

Reading On

Ephesians 2:6-7   Colossians 1:15

Acceptable in God's Sanctuary

SCRIPTURE READING: Psalm 15

KEY VERSES: Psalm 15:1-5

LORD, who may dwell in your sacred tent? Who may live on your holy mountain? The one whose walk is blameless, who does what is righteous, who speaks the truth from their heart; whose tongue utters no slander, who does no wrong to a neighbor, and casts no slur on others; who despises a vile person but honors those who fear the LORD; who keeps an oath even when it hurts, and does not change their mind; who lends money to the poor without interest; who does not accept a bribe against the innocent. Whoever does these things will never be shaken.

Who can enter God's sacred tent or sanctuary? David answers that question in today's verses by identifying 11 qualities of a person who is upright in deed, word, attitude, and finances. This righteous person:

1. walks blamelessly
2. does what is righteous
3. speaks the truth from his heart
4. has no slander on his tongue
5. does his neighbor no harm
6. casts no slur on others
7. despises evil people

8. honors those who fear the Lord

9. keeps his oath even when it hurts

10. lends his money without usury

11. doesn't accept a bribe against the innocent

These qualities don't come naturally to us. They are imparted to us by God through the Holy Spirit. But being blessed by God with these honorable characteristics doesn't mean we don't struggle with sin. We may look at a righteous person and think, *It must be easy for him to be a Christian. He apparently doesn't struggle with sin like I do.* But appearances can be deceiving. Living a righteous life comes when we choose to serve the Lord each day, and that's not easy for anyone. Living for God by living a righteous life depends on deciding, moment by moment, to do what is right. When we do our best and when we rely on His grace, we will be welcomed into His sanctuary.

> *Father God, thank You that I don't have to rely on my own resources to live a righteous life. Thank You for Your Spirit that teaches and transforms me. And thank You for David's words today. Help me to learn from what I've read and to live it out so that You will welcome me into Your sanctuary. Amen.*

Taking Action

- What does it mean to you to be in God's sacred tent or sanctuary?

- Choose one of the 11 points in today's psalm and decide what you will do to improve that area of your life this week. List specific actions, take the first step today, and note the results.

- What is your attitude toward worship? How regularly do

you attend worship services at church? Why does God call us to worship Him with His people?

Reading On

Psalm 27:5   Psalm 24:4

Joshua 24:14-15

"Where your treasure is, there your heart will be also."

Matthew 6:21

"Honey, Please Take Out the Trash"

SCRIPTURE READING: Philippians 2:1-11

KEY VERSE: Philippians 2:3
*Do nothing out of selfish ambition or vain conceit.
Rather, in humility value others above yourselves.*

Years ago Emilie and I had the good fortune to visit Canada and the town of Red Deer, a farming community on the flat plains of Alberta Province, halfway between Calgary and Edmonton. A delightful spot any time, but in winter the strong Arctic winds make the area very cold.

After landing at the airport and clearing customs, we were met by Val Day, one of our hostesses for the weekend. As she drove us north to Red Deer, she spoke modestly but with the unmistakable pride of a mother and wife about her children and her husband, Stockwell. She explained that her husband, who was in politics, would be home from the cabinet sessions in Edmonton over the weekend. That was the routine when the government was in session. Stockwell leaves home late Sunday afternoon, stays in his apartment in Edmonton through Thursday, drives back home to his Red Deer office Friday, spends the weekend with his family, and then starts all over again late Sunday afternoon.

I very much looked forward to meeting Stockwell B. Day, the Minister of Labor for Alberta Province. As the weekend neared, I heard all kinds of positive things about this very fine Christian politician. He was interviewed on television during the six o'clock news, and the newspaper printed several statements made by the Honourable Mr. Day during this session.

On Friday evening we were invited to the Days' home for dinner. After Emilie and I arrived and introductions were made, we enjoyed a barbecue on the patio with the Day family and other guests. Emilie and I knew we were in the home of someone special—but for other reasons than you might expect. This man was tremendously respected by the people in his province, but what impressed us more was that his family was a high priority for him. This man of God is the head of a family that lives out love. They share a sense of humor, appreciation of one another, and mutual respect. It was a pleasure to share the evening with them.

After Emilie's seminar on Saturday, Stockwell and Val drove us back to the airport so we could leave early Sunday morning. During the drive, I asked Stockwell a question that I often ask successful Christian men. "Stockwell, this week I've heard your name spoken with high admiration, I've seen the high regard your voters have for you, and I've heard you addressed by the title 'Honourable.' How do you stay humble and keep a proper perspective on who you are as a child of God?"

Without a moment's hesitation, Stockwell replied, "When I get home on Friday afternoon, I give Val a hug and then she very matter-of-factly says, 'Honey, please take out the trash.' With that simple request, I am back down to earth. I am reminded that I am a husband and father to a very special family before I am an Honourable Minister of Labor."

Friend, that's what it's all about! "Walk by the Spirit, and you will not gratify the desires of the flesh" (Galatians 5:16). We can have titles, fame, and wealth, but the Lord wants us, His children, to be humble in spirit.

Father God, thank You for making me who I am. I appreciate all that You've done for me and the many blessings You've given

*me. I want to stand before You humbly, recognizing that noth-
ing the world has given me should make me arrogant or high-
minded. Please give me a humble and serving spirit with my
family so that as I empty the trash, change diapers, and help in
the kitchen, I don't feel like less of a man. Amen.*

Taking Action

- How do you handle praise? Do you become self-righteous
  or are you able to remain humble?

- Do the people you work with consider you approachable?
  Why or why not? Is your humility or the lack of it a factor
  in how people view you?

- Do your children consider you a warm and approachable
  father? Why or why not? Is your humility or the lack of it a
  factor in their feelings about you?

- Does your wife believe you're sensitive and receptive? Why
  or why not? Is your humility or the lack of it a factor in her
  opinion?

- In what areas of your life do you need to be more humble
  in spirit?

- Choose one of these areas to work on this week. Write it
  down and commit to it.

Reading On

John 12:23-26   Job 42:1-6

Ephesians 5:21   Psalm 8

"Live by the Spirit, and you will not gratify
the desires of the sinful nature."

Galatians 5:16

A Tough-but-Tender Warrior

SCRIPTURE READING: 1 Thessalonians 2:1-16

KEY VERSES: 1 Thessalonians 2:7-8 NASB

*We proved to be gentle among you, as a nursing mother
tenderly cares for her own children. Having so fond
an affection for you, we were well-pleased to impart
to you not only the gospel of God but also our own
lives, because you had become very dear to us.*

When you think of the apostle Paul, you may think of the man who endured imprisonments, flogging, stoning, and shipwrecks (2 Corinthians 11:23-27). Toughness was very much a part of the fiery apostle. But his hard-as-nails toughness didn't mean he was without a tender side. Today's reading confirms he had one. He describes himself as being as gentle and tender as a loving mother is with her children.

I saw such an example of a tough-but-tender man when Barbara Walters interviewed American hero "Stormin' Norman" Schwarzkopf (1934–2012), the four-star general who led the multinational coalition forces of "Desert Storm" to victory and forced Iraq to relinquish its occupation of Kuwait (1991). As this tough military man talked about the war, I saw tears in his eyes. His interviewer noticed too and, in her classic style, Barbara Walters asked, "Why, General, aren't you afraid to cry?" General Schwarzkopf replied without hesitation, "No, Barbara. I'm afraid of a man who won't cry!"

This truly great man knew that being tough didn't mean being insensitive or unfeeling or afraid to cry. No wonder soldiers gave their best when they served under his command. They knew the general cared about them. They could trust the man giving their orders. We men want leaders whose hearts can be touched by our situations and who touch our hearts as well.

Even today I vividly remember the encouragement that my high school and college basketball coaches gave me when they called me to the sidelines. As the coach explained the next play or the strategy for a game-winning maneuver, he would put his arm on my shoulder. That simple touch said, "Bob, I believe in you. You can make it happen."

Athletics can indeed be a real source of encouragement as boys travel the path to manhood. Granted, professional sports have become larger than life with the influx of media dollars, but athletics remain a place where we can see the tender side of tough athletes. That's what we're looking at when we see grown men jump into the arms of a coach or a teammate, two or more buddies high-fiving it, or a swarm of players jumping on top of a player who just made a big play. This childlike excitement is the tender side of the not-to-be-beaten athlete.

Are you able to give your friends a pat on the back or a bear hug? We're all on the same team—God's team—and we all need some encouragement as we head onto the field to make the big plays. We need each other if we're going to be victorious in this game called life.

Father God, thank You for reminding me that it's okay to be tender at times. I'm glad Jesus is my example of toughness and tenderness. I know my family wants me to be more sensitive. They want me to take time to listen, to not be away from home so much, and to spend more time with them. And they'd probably even like me to be open enough to cry in front of them. I confess, Lord, that I am a husband and father who is often too occupied with my job and myself. Please help my family be patient with me even as You help me learn to be more tender with them. Amen.

Taking Action

- Plan and carry out a special evening with your wife. Romance her—not for your pleasure but to express your love for her.

- Spend some one-on-one time with each of your children. Go out for ice cream, play catch, or grab a Saturday breakfast. The plans don't need to be elaborate. The idea is to take time to get to know each one of them a little better.

- Ask each member of your spiritual support group what he does to express tenderness to his wife and children.

- Learn to give yourself to your family. Watch for needs and work to meet them without being asked.

Reading On

2 Corinthians 11:23-27   Ephesians 5:21

Titus 2:6-8   Philippians 3:17-21

Knowing What You
Need to Know

SCRIPTURE READING: Proverbs 1:1-7

KEY VERSE: Proverbs 1:7
*The fear of the LORD is the beginning of knowledge,
but fools despise wisdom and instruction.*

Most of what I really need to know about how to live, and what to do, and how to be, I learned in kindergarten. Wisdom was not at the top of the graduate school mountain but there in the sandbox at nursery school.

These are the things I learned: Share everything. Play fair. Don't hit people. Put things back where you found them. Clean up your own mess. Don't take things that aren't yours. Say you're sorry when you hurt someone. Wash your hands before you eat. Flush. Warm cookies and cold milk are good for you. Live a balanced life. Learn some and think some and draw and paint and sing and dance and play and work some every day.

Take a nap every afternoon. When you go out into the world, watch for traffic, hold hands, and stick together. Be aware of wonder.

Remember the little seed in the plastic cup. The roots go down and the plant goes up, and nobody really knows how or why, but we are all like that.

Goldfish and hamsters and white mice and even the little seed in the plastic cup—they all die. So do we.

And then, remember the book about Dick and Jane and the first word you learned, the biggest word of all: LOOK. Everything you need to know is in there somewhere. The Golden Rule and love and basic sanitation. Ecology and politics and sane living.

Think of what a better world it would be if we all—the whole world—had cookies and milk about three o'clock every afternoon and then lay down with our blankets for a nap. Or if we had a basic policy in our nation and other nations to always put things back where we found them and cleaned up our own messes. And it is still true, no matter how old you are, when you go out into the world it is best to hold hands and stick together.[5]

Robert Fulghum has a point when he says, "All I really need to know I learned in kindergarten." As true as it is that we gain fundamental lessons for life in kindergarten, King Solomon wisely tells us that "the fear of the LORD is the beginning of knowledge," the kind of knowledge we need for life now and life eternal.

In the book of Proverbs, Solomon offers advice on how to conduct ourselves in various situations in everyday life. His basic instruction is to fear and trust the Lord, and he challenges us to continually seek God's wisdom for the decisions we must make each day.

The kind of knowledge Solomon writes about goes beyond academic accomplishments to moral responsibility. It focuses on decision making and shows itself best in our self-discipline and moral living. It's far too easy, though, to raise our children to be lawyers, doctors, teachers, salespeople, or musicians rather than teaching them, first and foremost, to be good, moral, godly people. Our society and the world in general desperately need good people.

Fulghum offers great ideas, but we need God's ideas even more.

We need to base our notions of right and wrong on an accurate understanding of Scripture and a solid knowledge of God's commands to us. We aren't to be swayed by what the secular world says. God's Word tells us not to be conformed to the world, but to be transformed by the renewing of our minds (Romans 12:2). We must continually seek God's wisdom if we are to know His will for us, "his good, pleasing and perfect will" (Romans 12:2).

> *Father God, I want to be a man who seeks after Your knowledge. Show me Your ways that I might acknowledge You as God with how I live, what I choose, the words I speak, and the thoughts I think. Help me to understand that You are all I will ever need. Amen.*

Taking Action

- What decisions do you need to make today? On what basis will you make them—the world's teachings or God's Word?

- What can you do to get into the habit of looking to Scripture for guidance in your decisions and for answers to questions that come up?

- Do you have a verse of Scripture that serves as your theme for life? If not, ask God to give you one as you spend time in His Word this week. (I use Matthew 6:33 as mine.)

Reading On

Romans 12:1-2   James 3:13-18

Proverbs 3:1-18

Wisdom: Learn What the Bible Says

- King Solomon was the wisest man who ever lived. Read 1 Kings 3:3-28. Here Solomon asks for wisdom and God responds. What does this teach you about the nature and the value of wisdom?

- The book of Proverbs is a collection of wise sayings, most of which are attributed to King Solomon. Read Proverbs 1. What is the purpose of this book of wisdom? According to Proverbs 1:7 and James 1:5, how do we begin to acquire wisdom?

- The book of Proverbs repeatedly reminds us that God wants us to acquire wisdom. Look at Proverbs 16, especially verses 1-3, 9, 16, and 21-23. What guidelines do you find for wise living?

- James 3:13-18 describes two types of wisdom. Which type is evident in your own life? How do you know?

- The book of Proverbs has 31 chapters. Read one chapter each day and reflect on its teachings.

Have I Ever Seen a Christian?

SCRIPTURE READING: Psalm 78:1-7

KEY VERSE: Psalm 78:4

*We will not hide [God's commandments] from
their descendants; we will tell the next generation
the praiseworthy deeds of the LORD, his power,
and the wonders he has done.*

One evening, as a father was helping his young son get ready for bed, he talked about what Christians should be like and how they should act. When the father finished describing the attributes of a Christian, his son asked a startling question: "Daddy, have I ever seen a Christian?" The father was stunned. *What kind of an example have I been?* he wondered.

Imagine being asked that question by your son or daughter. Today's Scripture reading calls us to teach our children about God so clearly that they have no reason to wonder if they've ever seen a believer. The writer of Psalm 78 tells us to help our children know the things of God by telling them the many reasons we have to praise the Lord and teaching them His laws and statutes (verses 4-5). And such teaching happens as much—if not more—through our lives as through our words. Our children will look to us in the day-to-day situations of life to see what being a Christian looks like. That is one reason why God, speaking through Moses, instructs us to impress upon our children God's commandments by talking "about them when you sit at home and when you walk along the road, when you lie down and when you get up" (Deuteronomy 6:7).

It's a big order to fill. We fathers are to reflect God and His character to our children. As they look into our faces, listen to our words, and watch our lives, they are to see men of godly speech, actions, and goals. Granted, you and I are in process. Our Christian growth comes day by day as, with God's help, we take off the old self—those attitudes, beliefs, and behaviors that reflect the dark, sinful side of our nature—and are transformed by His Spirit into more Christlike people. Our children are watching this process. How are we doing? What are they seeing?

God calls us fathers to train and nurture our children in His ways, and that kind of teaching comes by our living example as well as by specific teaching times. When we ourselves are growing in our faith, we can reflect God's grace to our children, and they will know that they have seen a Christian.

> *Lord God, I thank You for the godly men You have put in my life who have modeled for me what being a follower of Christ is all about. They have been a real inspiration to my Christian growth. Help me to continually seek out such godly people who will live the Christian walk in front of me. And, Lord, help me be that kind of person in my own home. Be at work in my heart and mind to transform me so that I can better reflect You for my children in all I say and do. Amen.*

Taking Action

- Ask your children today what they think a Christian is. Learn from their response where you can sharpen your example. Make that area of your life a topic of your prayers and a focus of your efforts.

- Make thanksgiving the theme of a special time of prayer with your children. Let them hear you thank God for the blessings He has given you—and listen carefully to what they are thankful for.

■ Consider the decisions before you today. Where do you have an opportunity to do something of eternal significance? Write it down and do it!

Reading On

Ephesians 6:4   Deuteronomy 6:6-7

Ephesians 4:22-24

"The Lord is close to the brokenhearted and saves those who are crushed in spirit."

Psalm 34:18

A Friend Who Prays

SCRIPTURE READING: Colossians 1:9-12

KEY VERSE: Colossians 1:9
*Since the day we heard about you, we have not
stopped praying for you. We continually ask God to fill
you with the knowledge of his will through all the
wisdom and understanding that the Spirit gives.*

Have you discovered that geographic distance and passing years are ineffective obstacles for you and your real friends? It's true for me. Perhaps it's our common walk with the Lord that enables us to just pick up where we left off whenever we get together. Like the hidden-but-essential infrastructure of a building, these kinds of friends hold us up when challenges and trials come our way.

For me, prayer is an important part of friendship that lasts, and our passage today offers us an eloquent model of a Christian's prayer for his friends. Even though Paul had never visited the church of Colossae, his love for the people there was strong and ardent. As you read again today's Scripture, notice what a wonderful prayer it is for you to pray for your friends and for your friends to pray for you. Knowing that a friend is praying for me like this is a real source of encouragement and support.

If you aren't praying for your friends daily, let me suggest that Colossians 1:9-12 be your model. You'll be asking God to...

- give your friend the spiritual wisdom and understanding to know God's will

- help him "walk in a manner worthy of the Lord, [and] please Him in all respects" (verse 10 NASB)

- enable him to please God "by bearing fruit in every good work and increasing in the knowledge of God" (verse 10 NASB)

- grant him strength and power "for the attaining of all steadfastness and patience" (verse 11 NASB)

- thank God for all that He has given you—your friendship being one of those blessings (verse 12)

Now to which of your friends will you give the gift of this prayer? Tell your friend that you are praying for him each day, and let him know the specifics of your prayers. Let me assure you that it is a real comfort to have a friend praying for me like this—to know that he is asking God to enable me to honor Him in all I do, help me bear fruit for His kingdom, give me wisdom and understanding, and grant me strength, steadfastness, and patience.

By the way, these verses from Colossians are a good model for your prayers for your wife, other members of your family, your neighbors, and yourself. After all, every one of God's children needs to know His will, honor Him in all he does, grow in knowledge of the Lord, and be strong, steadfast, and patient as he serves Him.

Father God, thank You for blessing me with good friends. Thank You for this group of men who have helped shape my life. Without You and them, I wouldn't be who I am today. Help me be faithful in my prayers for them, their families, and their walks with You. Amen.

Taking Action

- Write down the names of one or two friends for whom you want to pray each day. Under their names, list several specific areas of concern.

■ Read Colossians 1:9-12 for 30 straight days. As you do so, pray for the friend(s) you listed.

Reading On

Ephesians 3:14-19   Philemon 1:4-7

"Trust in the LORD with all your heart and lean not on your own understanding; in all your ways submit to him, and he will make your paths straight."

Proverbs 3:5-6

Three Loves

Scripture reading: Deuteronomy 6:4-9

Key verse: Deuteronomy 6:5
Love the Lord your God with all your heart and with all your soul and with all your strength.

Today's Scripture reading talks about three basic loves—love of God, love of neighbor, and love of self. What a difference we Christians would make in the world if we were able to love this way! The passage goes on and challenges us to

- put these commandments in our hearts
- impress them on our children
- talk about them continually
- "tie them as symbols" on our bodies
- write them on our doorframes and gates

Clearly, this command to love is important to God. As we try to remain constantly aware of God's command, how do we live out these three loves? In his letter to the Ephesian church, Paul helps us answer that question by saying, "Be filled with the Spirit" (Ephesians 5:18).

If we are loving ourselves, we will speak and sing words of joy. Paul commands us to do just that when he continues, "speaking to one another with psalms, hymns, and songs from the Spirit. Sing and make music in your heart to the Lord" (verse 19). People able to love themselves, people comfortable with whom God made them to be, will have lives characterized by joy, praise, and enthusiasm. Are you able to reflect the joy of the Lord? That's one way to tell if you're able to love yourself.

If we are loving God, we will be able to fulfill the command of Ephesians 5:20 (NASB): "Always giving thanks for all things in the name of our Lord Jesus Christ to God, even the Father." If we love God, we will find reasons everywhere for giving Him thanks.

If we are loving other people, we will be able to "be subject to one another in the fear of Christ" (Ephesians 5:21 NASB). We will be less selfish and, therefore, more able to willingly set aside some of our needs in our relationships. We will let another person's needs take precedence over our own. This kind of submission (and that word has certainly taken a beating in our society) is to be based on reverence for God. As members of God's family, we submit to one another out of respect for God.

Together, the commands to love God with all our heart, all our soul, and all our strength and to love God, others, and ourselves are calls to put first things first. And it's a daily challenge to do so.

Father God, You know the demands on me as husband, father, and breadwinner. Help me to meet those challenges by starting each day with the question, "What can I do to love God with all my heart, soul, and strength today?" Help my relationships with others fall into place as I make loving You and loving them my goals. I want to better understand what kind of love You want me to have for myself. Your call to love seems so basic, but I know I'll be working at it my whole life. Amen.

Taking Action

- Write down several ways you presently live out your love for:

  - God

- others
- self

■ Now write down several new ways to love God, others, and yourself. Choose one in each category to start doing this week.

- God
- others
- self

Reading On

Ephesians 5:18-21   Matthew 22:36-40

Harmony in the Home

SCRIPTURE READING: Ephesians 3:14-21

KEY VERSES: Ephesians 3:17-19

I pray that you, being rooted and established in love,
may have power, together with all the Lord's holy people,
to grasp how wide and long and high and deep
is the love of Christ, and to know this love that
surpasses knowledge—that you may be filled to the
measure of all the fullness of God.

Sadly, many families today are characterized by disharmony. When that's the case in our homes, we do well to model our prayers for our family after Paul's words in today's reading. The things he prays for can lead to harmony:

- Pray that your family may be "rooted and established in love" (Ephesians 3:17). God's love can help us be patient and kind with one another. God's love is not envious, boastful, or proud. His love is not rude, self-seeking, or easily angered, and it does not keep track of wrongs. Furthermore, it protects, trusts, hopes, and perseveres (see 1 Corinthians 13:4-7). Isn't this the kind of love you want in your family? Then ask God to fill your home and your hearts with His love.

- Pray that each member of your family would be able "to grasp how wide and long and high and deep is the love of Christ" for him or her (Ephesians 3:18). Knowing

Christ's immeasurable love for us, knowing that He loves us just as we are, knowing that He made us special and unique, and knowing that He died for our sins enables us to love one another. May the members of your family begin to grasp the vastness of Christ's love for them, individually and collectively, so that they can more freely love each other.

- Pray that each family member would "know this love that surpasses knowledge" (verse 19). Because of our human limitations, such as they are, we cannot fully comprehend God's love for us, a love that let Jesus die for us. God's love is beyond our knowledge of human love. But accepting in faith this gracious love helps us live out the gospel in our life and in our family.

- Pray that each member of your family will "be filled to the measure of all the fullness of God" (verse 19). Each day I read God's Word, I learn more about His patience, mercy, forgiveness, joy, justice, kindness, compassion—the list goes on and on. Can you imagine being filled completely full with these characteristics of God? Can you imagine each member of your family being filled with these qualities? What a wonderful place your home would be! And that is what this prayer is all about!

I can't imagine a more relevant prayer for your family than these lines by the apostle Paul! Make Paul's prayer for the believers in Ephesus your prayer for your family and yourself, and then watch God work to bring harmony to your home.

Father God, You know the tensions in our family, and You know where we fail to love each other. I earnestly pray that You will work in our hearts to root and establish us in Your love. Help us realize how wide, how long, how high, and how deep

Your love for us is. I pray this for my family and for myself, that we will glorify You in our home. Amen.

Taking Action

- Make a point of telling each member of your family today that you love him or her.

- Do something to show a member of your family that you love him or her.

- Hugs are therapeutic. Your family members will be better at expressing love if they receive at least one hug a day. Get to work!

Reading On

Ephesians 4:29   Proverbs 24:3-4

James 1:22-23   James 2:15-17

We Do What We Want to Do

SCRIPTURE READING: Genesis 18:18-19

KEY VERSE: Genesis 18:19

*For I have chosen him, so that he will direct his children
and his household after him to keep the way of the LORD
by doing what is right and just, so that the LORD
will bring about for Abraham
what he has promised him.*

Lee Iacocca, former president of Ford Motor Company and CEO of Chrysler, shared this in his book *Talking Straight*:

> My parents spent a lot of time with me, and I wanted my kids to be treated with as much love and care as I got. Well, that's a noble objective. Everyone feels that way. But to translate it into daily life, we have to really work at it. There's always the excuse of work that gets in the way of the family. I saw how some of the guys at Ford lived their lives—weekends merely meant two more days at the office. That wasn't my idea of family life. I spent all my weekends *and* all my vacations with my wife and kids. Kathi was on the swim team for seven years, and I never missed a meet. Then there were tennis matches. I made all of them. And piano recitals. I made all of them too. I was always afraid that if I missed one, Kathi might finish first or finish last and I would

hear about it secondhand and not be there to congratu-late—or console—her.

People used to ask me: "How could somebody as busy as you go to all those swim meets and recitals?" I just put them down on my calendar as if I were seeing a sup-plier or a dealer that day. I'd write down: "Go to country club. Meet starts at three-thirty, ends four-thirty." And I'd zip out.[6]

Lee's quote reminds me that no matter what job or life we have, we all face many choices every day. We set our priorities by what we focus on and how we make those choices. To be sure that we're choosing what is most important, we need to reconfirm each day what is of greatest value to us. We also need to look to the Lord for His direction.

What are you doing to be directed by God? Do you have a teach-able spirit? Are you honestly seeking His will for you in the little details as well as the big issues of life? Ask God each day to help you choose to do what is right and just. We all do what we want to do, so ask Him to help you want to do His will. When you follow in His ways, the Lord will bring about for you what He has promised.

Today's key verse points out the reward of following God's ways in our family: again, that the Lord will bring about what He has promised. In Proverbs 24:3-4 we learn more about these prom-ises: "By wisdom a house is built, and through understanding it is established; through knowledge its rooms are filled with rare and beautiful treasures." Is the writer of Proverbs talking about fur-niture, carpets, crystal vases, and fine paintings? I don't think so. Instead, these rare and beautiful treasures God promises are God-fearing, God-respecting children with godly values who honor their mother and father and respect other people. God has promised these rewards and blessings if we follow His instructions.

Are you following God's instructions? What choices are you

making? What are you doing with your life? Ask God today to give you a new passion for following His directions and making His choices in your life.

> *Father God, let me build my house with wisdom, establish it with understanding, and through knowledge fill its rooms with rare and beautiful treasures—children who know You, love You, and serve You. Help me live so that my wife and children are a top priority in my life. Also give me a teachable spirit. Reveal to me today how I can live according to Your ways. Amen.*

Taking Action

- What specific instructions does God give you for raising your children? Write them down.

- Beside each God-given instruction you listed, state specifically what you plan to do to act on those instructions.

- List a few of the blessings God has so abundantly given you.

- A hundred years from now the size of your bank account won't matter, nor will the size or style house you live in or the model car you drive. But the world may be different because you were deeply involved in the lives of your children. Looking at your life from this perspective, what changes do you want to make?

Reading On

Proverbs 27:17	Proverbs 22:6
Proverbs 20:11	Proverbs 19:18

God's Rewards

SCRIPTURE READING: Matthew 19:27–20:16

KEY VERSE: Matthew 19:29-30
*Everyone who has left houses or brothers or sisters or father
or mother or wife or children or fields for my sake will receive
a hundred times as much and will inherit
eternal life. But many who are first will be
last, and many who are last will be first.*

Why do you do what you do? Through the years, I've asked myself again and again, "Why do I serve? What is my motivation for speaking, writing, giving to the church, being a father, and loving my wife and family?" Put more bluntly, "What will I get as a result of my efforts?"

You've probably asked the same questions. I know my employees did whenever I offered them promotions. Most would ask, "How much more money will I make?" and "Will there be any increase in health insurance, vacations, bonuses, retirement?" Basically they wanted to know, "What's in it for me?" And in today's Scripture passage, Peter asks Jesus the same question when he says, "We have left everything to follow you! What then will there be for us?" (Matthew 19:27).

In today's verses, Jesus answers Peter's question and tells him—and us—what's in it for us when we serve God and His kingdom:

- Whatever we give up we will receive a hundred times as much.

- We will inherit eternal life.
- Many who are first will be last, and many who are last will be first.

These rewards are gracious and generous, but are you letting these rewards motivate your service to God? Or do you, like many people, think instead that God will punish you if you don't serve Him? Each day I ask God to first reveal to me my true motivations in serving Him and then to purify my reasons. I ask Him to help me accept the rewards promised in His Word and serve because I love Him instead of fearing punishment. Do you believe that God graciously promises eternal life because we have accepted Jesus as Lord and Savior *and* gives us a hundredfold return on all we've given up to serve Him?

As the 1897 hymn by Johnson Oatman Jr. says, take a moment to "count your blessings, name them one by one." Some of the ones on my list include knowing Jesus face-to-face, my salvation, my family, a nice home, a worthwhile ministry, good health, our church, our pastor. And the list could go on and on, each item reminding me that God does indeed take care of His people when we sacrifice to serve Him.

Today's Scripture reading also teaches that "the last shall be first." You and I try hard to be fair in our dealings with people, and this passage can seem unfair from our human perspective. In one parable shared by Jesus, a farmer wants to give the man who was hired last the same pay he gave to workers who had been there longer (Matthew 20:14). Why would a farmer pay the late worker the same amount as the early worker who had been in the fields all day? The farmer here represents God, whose amazing grace and generosity know no bounds. It is irrelevant that we humans might feel the farmer's actions are wrong or unfair. God chooses to do what He chooses to do.

So are you willing to serve God? He will reward you generously whether you go to the field at three o'clock in the afternoon or have been there since early morning.

> *Father God, search me and show me my motivation for what I do. Forgive my selfishness. Give me a pure heart that joyfully and energetically serves You, the Author and Giver of life. Help me serve with my eyes on You and not on people hoping they'll notice what I do. And thank You, Lord, for the gracious and generous rewards You promise even when my motives aren't pure and my service is imperfect. Amen.*

Taking Action

- Answer the question that opens today's selection—"Why do you do what you do?"

- List at least 10 blessings. What does this list show you about God?

- Where is God calling you to serve? What will you do in response to His call?

Reading On

Matthew 6:33   Mark 10:29-31

Know Your Children

SCRIPTURE READING: Proverbs 22:1-16

KEY VERSE: Proverbs 22:6 NASB
*Train up a child in the way he should go, even
when he is old he will not depart from it.*

As I look at our grandchildren—Christine, Chad, Bevan, Bradley Joe II, and Weston—I see five unique people and find myself face-to-face with the challenge of understanding each of them so that I can help mold godly character in them. Fortunately, each of them wants to be known. In fact, each one of us—whatever our age—wants people to take time to know us, to appreciate how we're different from everyone else, and to recognize our likes, dislikes, and the things about us that make us who we are.

In raising our two children, Emilie and I saw a lot of differences between Jenny and Brad, and those differences are still there. Recognizing these differences early on, we realized we had to teach, motivate, and discipline each of them according to their personality. God helped us understand that children need to be trained in a way tailor-made for them.

The first word in today's key verse is the word *train*. In the Hebrew, this word originally referred to the roof of the mouth and the gums. In Bible times, the midwife would stick her finger into a sweet substance and then place it into the new baby's mouth to get the infant sucking. She would then hand the child to its mother, and the child would start nursing. This was the earliest form of "training." (We need to keep in mind, though, that the word *child* in today's text can be a newborn up through a person of marrying age.) The trick to get the baby nursing was only the first step in a long period of training.

According to the verse, the value of this training is so that "when he is old he will not depart from it." In Hebrew, this word for "old" means "bearded" or "chin." Solomon is talking about a young man who begins to grow a beard, and that can be as early as junior high or as late as college. The idea Solomon communicates is that we parents are to continue training our children as long as they are under our care—and we are to train our children God's way, not according to our ideas, our ways, or our plans.

It's important to see that this verse is not a guarantee to parents that raising children God's way means that they will never stray from His path. Our efforts to train our children to follow God will be most effective when we use the methods most appropriate to their unique personalities. We need to approach each child differently and not compare them to one another. We need to appreciate the fact that each child is uniquely made. We need to be students of our children.

It was easy to see that Jenny was not Brad and that Brad certainly wasn't Jenny. And like Jenny and Brad, each child has his or her own bent, already established by our Creator God when He places him or her in our family. God has given you unique children. Get to know them.

Father God, thank You for the children You've placed in my care. Help me to know each of them well. Give me insights into their unique personalities, patience so I can understand them, and wisdom to know how to teach them. Help me build them up to be all that You designed them to be. Amen.

Taking Action

- In what ways are your children different from you? Different from each other? Be specific.

- In light of the differences between your children you've

identified, how will you train them differently? What approach will you take with each one?

■ Learn one new thing about each of your children today. Then do something with that information.

■ Tell your child today one thing you appreciate about him or her that makes him or her special to you.

Reading On

Psalm 139:13-16

"In the day of my trouble I shall call upon You,
for You will answer me."

Psalm 86:7 NASB

The Language of Love

SCRIPTURE READING: 1 Corinthians 13:4-13

KEY VERSE: 1 Corinthians 13:4
*Love is patient, love is kind. It does not envy,
it does not boast, it is not proud.*

In 1987, our friend Bill Thornburgh was diagnosed with leukemia. Eighteen months and three rounds of chemotherapy treatment later, Bill went to be with our Lord. Soon afterward, when his wife, Carole, was getting ready to visit Bill's sister, Carole decided to take her some of Bill's old books. While sorting through them, Carole found an envelope addressed to her from Bill. He'd written Carole an Easter card two years earlier, and she'd tucked it away in a book. Rediscovering the card, she thanked God for her husband's written words. At Christmastime in 1989, Carole had this Easter message from her husband. It read:

A Tearful Week
A Long Week
A Hard Week
A Lonely Week
A Painful Week
A Revealing Week
A Recovering Week
A Reassuring Week
A Peace Week
A Rededication Week
A Friendship Week

A Love Week
A Roller Coaster Week
A Renewal Week
A Glorious Week
A Victorious Week
A Life-Changing Week
But a Week I Will Never Lose Sight of

May God be our source of true love and friendship. You have been so good these days. I love you for it. You have been all a husband would desire. Forgive me, Sweet, for not keeping our love fresh. I love you.

Happy Easter and Happy Beginnings,

Bill

Bill's words offered Carole a comforting sense of his presence after he was gone. But even when he was alive, Bill and Carole spoke openly of their love for one another. Do you and your wife? We husbands would do well to learn the language of love. We need to practice saying, "I love you." We need to say those words, but we also need to speak them through our sensitivity to our spouse, our actions, and our conversation. If I'm going to run some errands, for instance, I can ask Emilie if there's anything I can get for her while I'm out. Or I can let her know I'm listening to her by turning off the television or putting down the paper. I can also show Emilie that I love her with an evening at the theater, a new dress, a gift certificate for a dress, a pair of shoes, a massage, a weekend away—whatever would be a treat for her. However I choose to show my love, I say aloud to Emilie, "Just another way to say, 'I love you!'" Acts of kindness like this are powerful and effective ways to strengthen your friendship with your mate. Such thoughtfulness shows your wife that you do not take her for granted.

Emilie and I also rely on certain family rituals and traditions to give us opportunities to express our love for one another. We kiss each other goodnight and say, "May God bless your sleep." We celebrate our love on anniversaries and birthdays by giving each other small gifts. We telephone one another when we're apart, visit one of our favorite restaurants on special occasions, go out to lunch, attend the theater, and share hugs and (my contribution) corny jokes. All of these things—spontaneous little acts as well as carefully planned events—are ways to show your wife you love her.

One word of caution! Be sure you are expressing your love in the language—in the words and the actions—your *spouse* will understand as love! Just because you feel loved when she plans a special dinner doesn't mean that she feels loved when you do the same for her. Be a student of your wife. Know what best communicates to her the love you have. And keep your eyes open for common, everyday events that give you the chance to express that love.

I continually strive to make sure my love is patient, kind, that it does not envy, does not boast, or is not proud. It's a lifetime of challenges in developing a Christlike expression of love one to another.

Father God, I want my wife to know that I love her. Teach me to be more open about my feelings. Help me be a student of my wife so that I know what actions and words make her feel loved. Amen.

Taking Action

- Do something for your wife that you hate doing but she loves—watching a romantic movie or going shopping when your favorite ball game is on television.

- Send her flowers.

- Give her a certificate for a massage.

- Take care of the children while she goes on the church's women's retreat.

■ Go out for coffee with your wife and talk about the day.

Reading On

1 Peter 4:7-11   1 John 4:7-21

There's Something About that Name

SCRIPTURE READING: Isaiah 9:6-7

KEY VERSE: Isaiah 9:6

*He will be called Wonderful Counselor, Mighty God,
Everlasting Father, Prince of Peace.*

What do you think of when you hear the name "Jesus"? Miracles? Salvation? Peace? Purpose? Joy? Power? Hope? All of these—and more? There is indeed something about that name, the name of the Almighty God who parted the Red Sea, raised Lazarus from the dead, and lives today in every believer.

And the fact that He lives today gives us hope and peace. As Isaiah wrote, "Of the greatness of his government and peace there will be no end" (Isaiah 9:7). Life can bring sorrow, broken hearts, health problems, financial difficulties, and many other hardships. But God gives us peace and hope for those times. Let's depend on God and find refuge and restoration in Him.

It helps some people to think about putting all their problems and worries in a box, sealing the lid, laying it at Jesus' feet, and then walking away, never turning back. It also helps to realize that 80 percent of the things we worry about never happen anyway—and we can let Jesus take the remaining 20 percent. In response, He will give back to us 100 percent of His life and peace. In fact, He did it already for us when He hung on the cross of Calvary.

Jesus. There is indeed something about that name—and may you find in the Person it names exactly what you need today.

Father God, You have many names. As I search the Scriptures, teach me the significance of each one so that I can have a deeper understanding of who You are. Reveal Your character to me. Amen.

Taking Action

- What are you worried about today? What will you let Jesus do about these concerns?

- List your blessings one by one. What does this list reveal about God?

- Start a list of the various names of God. Add to it whenever you come across another one in your reading. Beside each of them, make a note of why that name is significant to you personally.

Reading On

Philippians 4:8   Psalm 23

Joshua 24:14-15

"Let the message of Christ dwell in you richly."

Colossians 3:16

A Child of God

SCRIPTURE READING: John 10:10-18

KEY VERSE: John 10:10
*The thief comes only to steal and kill and destroy;
I have come that they may have life,
and have it to the full.*

One evening Emilie and I attended a service at an Evangelical Free Church in Fullerton, California. Pastor Chuck Swindoll introduced the speaker for the evening—a man by the name of Ravi Zacharias. His opening statement was, "The most dangerous place for a young child today is in his mother's womb." He was talking about our country's abortion epidemic. Children are being thrown away like trash right in our own cities. We as a society no longer view children as "a gift of the LORD," much less a miracle of the almighty God (Psalm 127:3 NASB).

After a bout with cancer, our niece Becky and her husband, George, adopted a son. God allowed a child to be born to another woman so Becky and George could be parents. This child is another gift from God. He wasn't thrown away in an abortion clinic. Instead, he was adopted into a family who wanted a child. And that's exactly what God offers us. He wants to adopt us into His family. We are not God's throwaways. We are His much-loved children for whom He sent His Son Jesus to die. Jesus came to give us life, and then He went to the cross so that we will never have to suffer the punishment for our sin.

Jesus enables us to go before the almighty God, and our relationship with Him that Jesus makes possible fills the God-shaped void in our spirits. Nothing in the world can fill that vacuum—although we often try to fill it with work, recreation, busyness, toys, sex, alcohol, and many other things. We can experience this spiritual void as mental, emotional, and even physical problems. When those problems help us acknowledge the hunger for God that is at their root, we can find fulfillment, contentment, and the abundant life Jesus promised.

Have you let yourself be adopted as God's child? Are you experiencing the abundant life He offers His sons and daughters?

Thank You, Jesus, for showing me Your love by dying for me, a sinner. And thank You for the promise of abundant life. Help me to experience that even now. And, Lord, encourage me to view my children as gifts from You. Forgive me when I'm impatient with them and when I don't make them the priority I want them to be. Make me into the kind of father You want me to be. I pray all this for the sake of my children and You. Amen.

Taking Action

- Are you a child of God, adopted into His family through Jesus Christ? If you are, spend some time thanking God for what He did to make that possible. If not, ask Jesus into your heart and life now.

- Read the book of John in the New Testament. Get to know Jesus better.

- Pray that God will help you experience the abundant life He offers.

- Ask God how He wants you involved in fighting for the lives of unborn children in our country.

Reading On

John 1:9	Luke 9:23
Mark 9:37	John 1:12

"Delight yourself in the Lord;
and He will give you the desires of your heart."

Psalm 37:4 NASB

Wise and Loving Discipline

SCRIPTURE READINGS: Proverbs 3:11-12; 13:24; 15:13; 17:22; 22:15; 29:15

KEY VERSE: Proverbs 15:13
A happy heart makes the face cheerful, but heartache crushes the spirit.

Parenting is an overwhelming task, and knowing how to discipline our kids is one of the most perplexing aspects of the job. Fortunately, as you saw in today's Scripture reading, the book of Proverbs contains some specific verses that offer good biblical principles for raising children.

We often feel we are in a tug-of-war between child and parent. When the battle has worn us out, the natural tendency is to want to throw in the towel and give up. And far too often parents do in fact give up on the challenge of gently yet firmly shaping their child's will as a trainer would a wild animal or a potter would a piece of clay.

It takes godly wisdom to provide this kind of security for children. How do we set and maintain stable boundaries for them? First, we must note the difference between abuse and discipline. Proverbs 13:24 tells us that if we truly love our children, we'll discipline them diligently. Abuse is unfair, extreme, and degrading. Such action doesn't grow out of love; it springs from anger and hate. Abuse results in a child's damaged self-image, and that damage will often last a lifetime. Discipline, on the other hand, upholds the child's worth. It is fair and appropriate to the infraction.

Second, we must be sure the child understands the discipline he or she is to receive. When we disciplined Jenny and Brad, we spent a lot of time discussing with them what they did. We wanted to make sure they understood what the infraction was. On occasion when a sterner approach was necessary, we did give spankings. They were firmly applied to the beefy part of the buttocks, and they did hurt. Spankings were few and far between, though, and when they did occur, they were never given in anger. Afterward, we talked again with the children about why they were disciplined and how they would behave differently in the future.

One of the main purposes of discipline in our home was to have the children realize they were responsible for their actions and would be held accountable for their behavior. Since every child is different, the methods of discipline will vary according to temperament. (In our day, we didn't have "Time Out." However, we've found this to be a very good technique, and we used it with our grandchildren very effectively.) Whatever the type of discipline the infraction warranted, we always ended with prayer, warm hugs, and assuring words about how much we loved our child. This kind of correction strengthens a child's self-image. And clearly defining the boundaries adds to the child's sense of security. Our love for our kids—carefully communicated even in moments of discipline—motivated them to behave according to our family's standards of behavior.

Third, when we discipline our children, we want to shape and not crush their spirit. As Proverbs 15:13 teaches, you can tell by looking into the eyes of children those who are being crushed and those being firmly but lovingly shaped. Our goal as parents is to provide our children with solid direction and self-assurance that will see them through life. The child who is shaped with loving and firm discipline will have a love for life, but a child whose spirit has been crushed has no hope for the future.

Fourth, our discipline must be balanced. We don't want to be so rigid that we don't allow our kids to make mistakes or so loose that they are bouncing off the walls trying to find the boundaries.

Children must know where the boundaries are and what the consequences are if they choose to go beyond these limits.

Fifth, as you discipline your children, be consistent in your approach. Here are some guidelines:

- Make sure there is a clear understanding of the rules.
- Discipline in private. If you're in a public setting, wait until you can be alone.
- Review the infraction and its consequences.
- Be firm in your discipline.
- Assure your child of your love and concern.
- Hug your child after each disciplinary moment.
- End your session with a time of prayer. (Give your child an opportunity to pray too.)

As Emilie and I look back over our child-raising years, we realize that we made plenty of mistakes. But when we did, we tried always to admit them to our children. Even though you'll miss the mark occasionally, be sure that you are moving in the proper direction of discipline administered in love. Know that your children want to know their boundaries. Setting and enforcing clear boundaries is a gift of love to them that results in security and self-assurance they can carry through life.

> *Father God, You know that I want for my children what's best for them. Give me the patience to get to know each of my children individually. Grant me the wisdom to know what kind of discipline will be most effective for each one. Help me be an effective father who is able to train my children to love and serve You. Amen.*

Taking Action

- Do you have a clear direction regarding the goal of your

children's discipline? If not, spend some time today thinking about it. Write down some of your ideas. If you're married, you may want to review these ideas with your mate.

▪ Tell each member in your family today that you love them and give a few reasons why.

▪ Take a poll tonight at dinner. Ask each family member, "What's the best thing that happened to you today?" The answers will give you some insights into your children. (Parents must participate too!)

Reading On

Mark 12:28-31	1 Peter 5:5-6
Galatians 5:16	Colossians 3:17

"As the heavens are higher than the earth,
so are my ways higher than your ways,
and my thoughts than your thoughts."

Isaiah 55:9

"I Didn't Believe It Anyway"

SCRIPTURE READING: John 6:35-40

KEY VERSE: John 6:40

*My Father's will is that everyone who looks to
the Son and believes in him shall have eternal life,
and I will raise him up at the last day.*

Emilie and I arrived at our hotel after flying from California to Hartford, Connecticut. It was our first holiday seminar for the season, and the church put us up at a beautiful Ramada Inn. We were anxious to see the turning of the leaves in the East for the first time, and they were at their peak in early October. We registered at the hotel and went directly to our room. After the airport waits, plane layovers, delays, cramped seating, and heavy luggage, we just wanted to sleep. We turned off the lights at about 9:30 in the evening.

Two-and-a-half hours later we were awakened by what we thought was a smoke alarm. I picked up the phone to call the front desk while Emilie looked out the peephole in the door. She couldn't see any smoke, and I wasn't getting an answer from the front desk. As I let the phone ring and ring, the alarm got louder. When Emilie looked out the peephole again, she saw a man running down the hall pulling his pants and jacket on. "Bob, it's a fire!" Emilie yelled. "People are evacuating the building."

I quickly hung up, threw on some clothes, grabbed our briefcases, and left the room. By now, many other guests were doing the same. The alarm was still blasting, and we heard sirens from the fire trucks heading for the hotel. As we walked toward the stairs to hurry down six flights, people pushed through to get ahead. One lady kept yelling, "Hurry, Ruth! Hurry, Ruth!" But Ruth just couldn't move as fast as the others.

We finally made it out into the very chilly, 34-degree midnight air. The entire hotel had been evacuated onto the street, and firefighters were everywhere—only to find out it was a false alarm. We all headed back to our rooms. As we got off the elevator on our floor, a little lady opened the door to her room just enough to look out and ask, "Was it a fire?"

"False alarm," we answered.

"Well, I didn't believe it anyway," she said.

Crawling back into bed, Emilie and I realized how that woman's words echoed the feeling of so many people at Jesus' first coming—"I didn't believe it anyway." How many people heard the message, saw Jesus, witnessed His miracles—and still didn't believe?

The message is clear today: Jesus lives! The Bible tells us the truth about God's plan for salvation, Jesus' role in that plan, and the response to that plan that leads to eternal life. Today's Scripture reading tells us to believe and we will receive eternal life. But today—like 2000 years ago—many people say, "I don't believe it." One day it will be too late to choose to believe.

Father God, You know where my heart is hard toward Your message and hard toward You. Forgive me and work in me to soften those places. Give me the simple faith of a young child. Let me set aside the sophistication and doubts of adults. And, Lord, give me the enthusiasm of a young child that I may share the gospel message with others so they might come to believe in You. Amen.

Taking Action

■ Share with a friend how you came to believe in Christ.

■ How do you show others that Jesus lives? Consider how
your actions also reflect Jesus alive in you.

Reading On

2 Timothy 3:16   Acts 13:38-39

Finding Favor in God's Eyes

SCRIPTURE READING: Genesis 6:8-22

KEY VERSES: Genesis 6:8,22

Noah found favor in the eyes of the LORD...
Noah did everything just as God commanded him.

If you were to pick up today's paper, you'd probably find a story about someone being honored for something he or she did. The accomplishment of someone in government, sports, medicine, education, theater, or music being acknowledged by peers or even the world in general is common. Man finding favor with man isn't unusual. But have you ever thought about how much richer it would be to have *God* find favor with you? It's awesome to think of our holy God finding favor in us human beings, but He does. And today's reading gives us an example.

Noah lived in a sin-filled world much like ours today. (We human beings haven't changed much over the centuries—we just call sin something else.) Despite the wickedness around him, Noah lived a godly life that was pleasing to God. It's important to realize that Noah found favor not because of his individual goodness but because of his faith in God. You and I are judged by that same standard. Are we faithful and obedient to God?

Although Noah was upright and blameless before God, he wasn't perfect. *Genuine faith* is not always perfect faith. Despite his human failings, Noah walked with God (Genesis 6:9). The circumstances of Noah's life could have blocked his fellowship with God, but his devoted heart qualified him to find favor with God.

Are you seeking favor with God or the favor and honor of human beings? Noah wanted to please God. Know that when you go to God and admit that you are a sinner, you are pleasing God. At that time, you find His grace and move into a closer relationship with Jesus Christ. May you take steps as Noah did to find favor in God's sight.

> *Father God, what an honor for Noah to have found favor in Your eyes. Help me be faithful and obedient to You so that I too will find favor with You. Give me a renewed hunger for Your Word so that I will know what You want from me. Show me how to be faithful to Your commands. Amen.*

Taking Action

- What can you do to find favor in God's eyes? What kind of person can you be to find favor in His eyes?

- If you don't think your life finds favor with God, what changes do you want to make? What steps will you take— and what step will you take today?

- What will you do to know God's Word better? Who will you find to hold you accountable to obeying God's Word?

Reading On

John 3:16   Philippians 2:12-15

James 4:6   Psalm 19:14

Speak Out!

SCRIPTURE READING: Romans 1:1-17

KEY VERSE: Romans 1:16

*I am not ashamed of the gospel, because it is the power
of God that brings salvation to everyone who believes:
first to the Jew, then to the Gentile.*

Ashamed of the gospel of Christ! Let the skeptic, let the wicked profligate, blush at his deeds of darkness, which will not bear the light, lest they should be made manifest; but never let the Christian blush to own the holy gospel. Where is the philosopher who is ashamed to own the god of Nature? Where is the Jew that is ashamed of Moses? or the Moslem that is ashamed of Mohammed? and shall the Christian, and the Christian minister, be ashamed of Christ? God forbid! No! Let me be ashamed of myself, let me be ashamed of the world, and let me blush at sin; but never, never, let me be ashamed of the gospel of Christ![7]

Dr. R. Newton was passionate in his cry. We who name Jesus our Lord and Savior should never be ashamed of the gospel! The apostle Paul certainly never hesitated to share the gospel—and at far greater risk than you and I can imagine. In today's reading, the apostle sets forth seven principles about the gospel. Getting these down can help you and me be bolder in our witness for God's good news.

Point I: We are "set apart for the gospel" (verse 1). How can that truth help you establish your daily priorities? It's not family, work, finances, politics, or sports that goes to the top of the list. It's the gospel—the love and forgiveness of God made manifest in the birth, life, and death of Jesus Christ—that is to be the focus and guiding principle for your day.

Point II: This gospel was "promised beforehand through his prophets in the Holy Scriptures" (verse 2). The gospel we are commanded to share with those who have never heard it is rooted in history, and that history is documented in the Bible. Our faith is not something recently thought up by a group of people in a back room.

Point III: We are to share the gospel with our whole heart (verse 9). With a passion greater than our zeal for the hometown team, we are to share the news of Jesus Christ with our family, friends, neighbors, and acquaintances.

Point IV: We are to share this good news with everyone (verses 14-15). Paul says he was obligated and eager to preach this gospel to both the Greeks and non-Greeks, to the wise and to the foolish, to everyone. And we are to follow Paul's example. The message of Jesus can make a difference in anyone's life.

Point V: We are to take a stand for the gospel (verse 16). Paul forcefully states, "I am not ashamed of the gospel." Can you and I say the same? We need to stand strong in and for our faith, unashamed of the One who died for our sins and was willing to love and serve as He did.

Point VI: We need to see the power of the gospel for salvation (verse 16). The gospel of Jesus Christ is an agent of change. He alone gives real purpose and meaning to life. He alone can help us find victory in our struggle against the power of sin. He alone can transform and heal us. Each of us needs to share our personal experience of these truths.

Point VII: We are to live a life of righteousness by faith (verse 17). When we study the gospel, the righteousness of God is revealed to us so that we can go out and live a righteous life by the power of the Holy Spirit.

Do you "blush to own the gospel"? Do you hesitate to talk about Jesus and the salvation He offers us? Today's passage gives several reasons to speak out. Let's do so!

> *Father God, give me renewed passion for You and Your gospel truth. Don't let me take for granted the freedom I have to share the gospel. Help me not rely on others to do the sharing. You know the reasons I hesitate. Help me overcome them. Give me boldness when I have an opportunity to tell someone about You and Jesus. Amen.*

Taking Action

- Read a good biography of some people of faith who have gone before you. Where do you see the power of the gospel in their lives?

- Whom in your life have you wanted to share the Good News with? Do it!

- What can you do to be more aware of opportunities to share the gospel? What can you do to prepare yourself to take advantage of those opportunities?

- Thank God for sending Jesus Christ to fulfill the prophecies of the Old Testament. Thank God for your salvation.

Reading On

2 Timothy 3:16	1 Corinthians 15:1-6
Luke 24:27-32	Hebrews 11:1

Live for Today

SCRIPTURE READING: Romans 15:5-13

KEY VERSE: Romans 15:13

*May the God of hope fill you with all joy and peace
as you trust in him, so that you may overflow
with hope by the power of the Holy Spirit.*

It seems we spend so much time fretting about what we didn't do yesterday and worrying about tomorrow that we forget the only day that counts—today! One of the Barnes' mottos is "85 percent of the things we worry about never come true." Consider how much energy, focus, time, and effort you surrender to those hypothetical problems. Then imagine how much you could accomplish if only you put that same energy toward prayer, family time, and positive actions.

As soon as we trust God with our lives, we can live with peace in the moment.

There are many advantages to this perspective and attitude adjustment. When we stay positive and do not dwell on those things we cannot control, we are better able to serve God and the church body. We can set aside what doesn't matter, and we can fix our attention on what does. We can turn to our brothers and sisters in Christ and be an uplifting presence. "May the God who gives endurance and encouragement give you the same attitude of mind toward each other that Christ Jesus had, so that with one mind and one voice you may glorify the God and Father of our Lord Jesus Christ" (Romans 15:5-6).

You will discover great joy when you allow yourself to focus on what God gives you to tend to each day. There is more time and more motivation to stop and smell the roses, hear the train whistle, gaze at the clouds passing overhead, listen to the sound of rain falling on the roof, or watch the sunset and marvel at God's handiwork.

Discover the power of experiencing every minute of every day. The moment you do, you will have renewed awe for all God creates, makes happen, and shares with His children.

In this very moment, praise the Lord for the gift of life, and share your gratitude with others.

Father God, You created this moment so that I could experience the joy of living. Help me to live with a sense of wonder. Release me from the worries that occupy my thoughts. I want to live today with You in a new way. I am grateful for all that You have given to me. Help me to turn my joy and gratitude into actions to serve Your children and bring You glory. Amen.

Taking Action

- Do something today that a child would do. Buy an ice cream cone. Skip a pebble across the pond. Fly a kite at the beach. Spend time with a friend and share with them the encouragement you have found in Christ.

- Every morning, choose to dedicate that day to God and His purpose. Leave a note on your mirror to remind you to live in the now.

Reading On

Philippians 4:13   Hebrews 11:23-28

Matthew 6:25-34

The Roots of Humility

Scripture reading: Philippians 2:1-8

Key verse: Philippians 2:5
*In your relationships with one another,
have the same mindset as Christ Jesus.*

Have you heard of the pastor who was given a badge for being the most humble person in the church? The badge was taken back when he wore it!

Humility. It's hard to get a handle on it. What exactly is it?

I stood in the upstairs hallway, looking down over the bannister and waiting for the younger children to come in for their baths. My oldest daughter, taking a piano lesson, was in the living room directly below, and the repetitive melody she was playing echoed through my mind.

I noticed, however, that one of my young sons was trudging slowly up the stairs, head bowed, grubby hands covering his small, dirt-streaked face. When he reached the top, I asked him what was wrong.

"Aw, nothing," he replied.

"Then why are you holding your face in your hands?" I persisted.

"Oh, I was just praying."

Quite curious now, I asked what he was praying about.

"I can't tell you," he insisted, "because if I do, you'll be mad."

After much persuasion I convinced him that he could confide in me and that, whatever he told me, I would not get mad. So he explained that he was praying about a problem he had with his mind.

"A problem with your mind?" I asked, now more curious than ever, wondering what kind of problem a child of six could have with his mind. "What kind of problem?"

"Well," he said, "you see, every time I pass by the living room, I see my piano teacher, and my tongue sticks out."

Needless to say, it was hard to keep a straight face, but I took his problem seriously and assured him that God could, indeed, help him with it.

Later, on my knees beside the bathtub as I bathed this little fellow, I thought how I still struggle with the problem of controlling my mind and my tongue. That afternoon as I knelt to scrub that sturdy little body, the tub became my altar; the bathroom, my temple. I bowed my head, covered my face, and acknowledged that I, like my son, had a problem with my mind and tongue. I asked the Lord to forgive me and to give me more and more the mind and heart and attitude of Christ.[8]

With the media constantly bombarding us with messages about self-esteem, it's easy to be confused about what genuine humility is. Having the mind and heart and attitude of Christ is a good start, and verse 3 in today's passage adds this: "Do nothing out of selfish ambition or vain conceit. Rather, in humility value others above yourselves."

As we study the life of Christ, we see that His willingness to serve had its roots in His confidence that God loved Him. Jesus found strength and security in knowing how valuable He was to His Father.

The knowledge of His Father's love enabled Jesus to serve people and ultimately die for us sinful human beings. Likewise, knowing our value to God is the first step toward true humility.

It's out of strength, not weakness, that we grow in humility. Dr. Bruce Narramore says that humility has three elements:

- recognition that you need God
- a realistic evaluation of your abilities
- a willingness to serve[9]

Are those three elements in place in your life? They are aspects of humility and, therefore, key to serving God.

> *Father God, You know how self-centered I am. You know how I'm always busy with something and hate to be inconvenienced. I need to learn to give myself to others. Teach me humility and how to serve as Christ did. Amen.*

Taking Action

- Do you recognize your need for God? If so, thank God for that awareness. If not, why not?

- Evaluate your abilities. List 10 strengths and 10 weaknesses. What are you going to do for the kingdom of God with your strengths? What plans do you have for turning your weaknesses into strengths?

- In what three capacities or organizations would you be willing to serve? Step forward and volunteer your services in one of those areas this week.

Reading On

Philippians 2:8-9   James 1:26–3:18

Psalm 39:1-13

Under Orders

SCRIPTURE READINGS: Ephesians 5:21-33;
1 Corinthians 11:2-12

KEY VERSE: 1 Corinthians 11:3
*I want you to realize that the head of every man
is Christ, and the head of the woman is man,
and the head of Christ is God.*

Y ou and I are under orders. The Lord of the universe has called us into His service as husbands to our wives and fathers to our children, and in doing so He describes a man's role in the home as "head." That concept is His choice, not ours. The New American Standard Version puts it this way: "Christ is the head of every man, and the man is the head of a woman, and God is the head of Christ." These orders—found in God's Word—have been delivered, once and for all. We men are not asked to lead; we are *commanded* to lead. It's not an option.

Throughout the Bible, we find God's instructions to those under authority—to anyone who is governed, including believers in the church, wives, children, servants, employees, and yes, husbands. And God's instructions to all are very clear. We are to

- be subject to Christ
- be subject to one another
- respect one another

The world tells us, "You are your own boss. You're not accountable

to anyone. Do what you want to do. And be sure people bow to you."
But that is not the message of Scripture. We men do have a certain amount of authority, but more importantly, we men are under
authority. We are under the authority of Jesus Christ. And if we are
to please the One who gives us our orders for life, we have to ask ourselves questions like these:

- Am I loving my wife as myself?

- Am I taking into account her ideas, opinions, and
  thoughts; her needs, desires, and dreams?

- Are my children responding positively to my leadership
  style?

- Are they able to talk to me? Do I respect them and show
  them that respect? Do my children respect me?

- Am I respectful and submissive to God, to my pastor, to
  civil authority, and to other believers?

Before you and I can ever lead the way God wants us to, we
must learn to follow Him in all we do. Only then can we be effective leaders in our homes—leaders who encourage our wives and
children in their spiritual growth and care for their emotional and
physical needs.

As you consider these orders, hear what Susanna Wesley, the
mother of Methodist leader John Wesley, said: "There are two things
we have to do with the gospel: one is to believe it. The second is to
live it." If we don't live out our faith in the One who is our Head, our
leadership will fail. Put differently, if we aren't under God's authority, then we cannot be effective in authority. No one wants to follow
a leader who is selfish. After all, when we're self-centered, we can't be
God-centered.

*Father God, may I be content to live under Your author-
ity. Give me a heart that is submitted to You so that I will*

hear Your wisdom for leading with godly authority. Teach me through Your Word and through Christians leaders how to make You number one in my life. Only then can I lead my family in the way You've called me to. Amen.

Taking Action

- What does it mean to you in your day-to-day life to be a man under authority?

- Discuss 1 Corinthians 11:3 and the idea of "headship" with your wife. Take the risk of asking her, "What do I need to do to be a better leader?"

- Take one of your children out for breakfast on Saturday and ask what you can do to be a better dad. Take the risk of being transparent and open to suggestions.

Reading On

Romans 5:12-16   Matthew 20:20-28

Matthew 19:3-9   Genesis 2:24-25

"We live by faith, not by sight."

2 Corinthians 5:7

Be Still

SCRIPTURE READING: Psalm 46

KEY VERSE: Psalm 46:10
*Be still, and know that I am God; I will be exalted
among the nations, I will be exalted in the earth.*

B e still, and know that I am God." Easier said than done, isn't
it? It's hard to find a quiet moment in the day—a few minutes
to relax and think and pray. We're constantly on the move, pres-
sured by the demands of work and family and whatever church
involvement, community activities, and recreation we try to fit in.
Still moments with God just don't happen with full schedules. So
what's the answer? I've found that I have to make appointments
with myself if I am to create opportunities to rest, plan, regroup, and
draw closer to God. Perhaps the same is true for you too.

As I write these words, Emilie and I are at a retreat in Laguna
Beach, California. It's July, and the temperature is 83 degrees. The
weather is perfect, and there's something calming about the waves
crashing on the shore. We've spent four days resting and reading.
This afternoon we've talked about family, ministry, food, goals,
God's love, His Word, and our writing endeavors. Now we're both
quiet, and I'm feeling that rare sense of stillness that the psalmist
talks about.

It's not often I'm still like this. My life isn't in balance the way
I think it should be. I'm more outwardly focused than inwardly
focused. Goals and deadlines, coping with stress, taking care of daily

chores, handling retirement finances, getting things done—I spend more time and energy on these things than I do praying, meditating on God's Word, listening for His direction, dreaming, and just being with God.

When I was younger, I was pulled in a lot of different directions, but as I've gotten older, I find myself doing more of the inward things. I want to glorify God with my life. I want to spend more time alone with Him. I want to get to know Him better. I want Him to use me. I want to know His peace. And you probably want those things for yourself as well. After all, regular down times—the psalmist's stillness—are as important and necessary as sleep, exercise, and healthy food. But, again, who has the time?

Well, Satan sure doesn't want us to take the time to be still with God. And the devil doesn't make it easy for us to eliminate the distractions of the job, stress from the boss, family responsibilities, ringing phones, and doing what the kids need. Emilie and I know the battle to make time for rest. So when we set up the year's calendar, we set aside blocks of time to be alone and quiet. In between the speaking engagements, interviews, and travel, we make time for quiet. Our marriage needs it. Our walk with God needs it.

Emilie talks about the door to stillness. And she's right. It's there waiting for any of us to open, but it won't open by itself. We have to *choose* to turn the knob and make time to enter and sit a while. Each one of us needs to learn to balance the time we spend in quiet and calm with the time we spend in the fray of everyday existence. Ecclesiastes 3:1 says, "There is a time for everything"—and that includes a time to be still despite our busy lives.

> *Father God, life is moving much too fast. The demands never let up, and the pressures never ease. I struggle to take a time out. I know I'm more relaxed and can better serve You as man, husband, father, and worker when I have a daily time with You. Show me how to make that time happen. Amen.*

Taking Action

- Read Ecclesiastes 3:1-8. What time in life is it for you right now?

- If you find it difficult to develop a habit of quiet time, find a prayer partner with the same problem and hold each other accountable.

- What will you do to cut down the busyness of your life? What distractions will you eliminate?

Reading On

Isaiah 30:15   Psalm 116:7

"Do not love the world or anything in the world.
If anyone loves the world,
the love of the Father is not in them."

1 John 2:15

Stories to Share

SCRIPTURE READING: Philippians 1:3-11

KEY VERSE: Philippians 1:3
I thank my God every time I remember you.

On an unusually warm, sunny January day many years ago, two of our grandchildren came to visit. Ten-year-old Christine helped her Grammy Em cook dinner. Bevan and I raked the garden and picked oranges, avocados, and lemons off the trees that surrounded our house. As the afternoon progressed, we working men got hot and tired. We were really glad to see Emilie and Christine come up the hill with juice and snacks. We thanked them and headed for the bench that sits under a large, shade-giving avocado tree overlooking the grounds and the street in front of our house.

That night, Emilie and I talked about our day with the grandchildren. "What do a PaPa and seven-year-old grandson talk about on a bench under a big avocado tree?" Emilie asked.

"Oh," I replied, "boys talk just like you girls talk—but about boy things."

I'd told Bevan, "Someday when PaPa's in heaven and you drive down this street as a man, you'll look at this bench we are sitting on and remember the day that Grammy Em and Christine served us jam and toast with a glass of juice."

Then Bevan said, "Not only will I remember, but I'll bring my son, and someday he'll bring his son and point to the bench and tell him about the toast and jam we ate on the bench under that big avocado tree over there."

At only seven years old, Bevan already understood something of the value of one generation sharing stories with the next. What a privilege and responsibility we parents have! We're called to teach our children and grandchildren the story of God's love, the stories of Jesus, so that someday they will thank God for their memory of us and the stories we shared.

> *Father God, thank You for the story of salvation—for giving Your Son for my sins. Give me Your words and genuine enthusiasm as I tell that story to my children so they will come to know and serve You. And one day they'll tell their own children about You and Your Son! Amen.*

Taking Action

- What stories from your father and grandfather do you especially value?

- What stories do your children or grandchildren like you to tell again and again? (If your list is short, turn to the Bible to add to your repertoire!)

- Take a walk with a child. Listen to the stories that he or she has to tell.

Reading On

1 Corinthians 1:4   Deuteronomy 6:7

Psalm 67:1-2

The Heat of Life

Scripture reading: Job 23:1-12

Key verse: Job 23:10

*[God] knows the way that I take; when
he has tested me, I will come forth as gold.*

When times are hard, it's easy to ask, "Why, Lord? Why do Your children suffer?" Job certainly had every reason to ask that question. He loved and obeyed God, but God gave Satan permission to test him. That meant great suffering and loss for Job, but he was a man with staying power. One reason his faith in the Lord didn't waver was because his masculinity wasn't determined by what he owned, the size of his home, the amount of his investments, what he could do, the people he knew, the model of donkey he rode, or his status in the community. Job's masculinity and personhood were firmly rooted in who he was, alone and naked, before God. And God is what makes men of all of us.[10]

In that process, God often uses suffering. Our friends Glen and Marilyn Heavilin, for instance, know the kind of suffering Job knew. They have lost three sons—one in a crib death, one twin by pneumonia a few weeks after he was born, and the second twin was killed at age 17 by a teenage drunk driver. Glen and Marilyn were tested, but they have come through it like gold from a refiner's fire. Today they use their experiences to glorify the name of the Lord.

Marilyn's first book, *Roses in December,* was the story of how they lost their sons. Marilyn has had the opportunity to speak all over the country in high school auditoriums filled with teenagers. There she shares her story and talks about life and death, chemical dependency, and God.

Did God know what He was doing when He chose the Heavilins? Of course. They persevered and shine as gold for Him. Their pain will never be gone, but they still go forth and minister to others. They've been very active in Compassionate Friends, a support group for families who have experienced the death of children. God knew the path the Heavilins would take when they faced their tragic losses, and He's been there with them as their faith in Him has been purified.

Every one of us has experienced some kind of tragedy. It's not the specifics of the event that matter as much as how we handled it. Today many support groups exist in churches and the community to help us deal with the losses we face. A church in Southern California, for instance, has a large group for people who are chemically dependent and their families, and God has used these weekly meetings to change lives. People are talking about their pain and praying together, and many are coming forth as refined gold. Emilie and I have also visited a church in Memphis, Tennessee that started a support group for homosexuals. Many who attend are leaving the gay lifestyle and coming forth as refined gold as well.

Whatever loss you're dealing with and however you're being tested, you can be sure that others have been tested that way too. So don't go through the testing alone. God is with you! He may also help you find someone through your church who will support and encourage you. You too can come forth as refined gold.

Father God, it's hard to want to be tested to become more like Your Son, Jesus Christ. But I know from experience that I rarely grow during the good times. It's the heat of life that makes my faith shine like refined gold. When the fires come, Lord, help me remember that You are with me. Amen.

Taking Action

▪ What pain and/or test are you experiencing today?

▪ In a prayer or a letter, let God know how you feel.

▪ How might God be using this in your life to help your faith "come forth as gold"? Be specific.

▪ Find out if there's a support group that could help you. Make a phone call or go online to find out more about it. The next step is to attend a meeting.

Reading On

Psalm 66:10   2 Corinthians 4:7-9

Psalm 51:10

"Carry each other's burdens,
and in this way you will fulfill the law of Christ."

Galatians 6:2

Being a Friend

SCRIPTURE READING: 2 Timothy 1:16-18

KEY VERSE: 2 Timothy 1:18

You know very well in how many ways
[Onesiphorus] helped me in Ephesus.

In his second letter to Timothy, the apostle Paul writes about One-siphorus, a man who was a special friend. He had "often refreshed" Paul and wasn't ashamed of Paul being in chains. Onesiphorus searched hard for Paul until he found him! Onesiphorus is the kind of friend we all need. And so is Pythias. Read his story:

> Damon was sentenced to die on a certain day, and sought permission of Dionysius of Syracuse to visit his family in the interim. It was granted, on condition of securing a hostage for himself. Pythias heard of it, and volunteered to stand in his friend's place. The king visited him in prison, and conversed with him about the motive of his conduct; affirming his disbelief in the influence of friendship. Pythias expressed his wish to die that his friend's honor might be vindicated. He prayed the gods to delay the return of Damon till after his own execution in his stead.
>
> The fatal day arrived. Dionysius sat on a moving throne, drawn by six white horses. Pythias mounted the scaffold and calmly addressed the spectators: "My prayer is heard: the gods are propitious; for the winds have been contrary till yesterday. Damon could not come; he could

not conquer impossibilities; he will be here tomorrow, and the blood which is shed today shall have ransomed the life of my friend. Oh! could I erase from your bosoms every mean suspicion of the honor of Damon, I should go to my death as I would to my bridal. My friend will be found noble, his truth unimpeachable; he will speedily prove it; he is now on his way, accusing himself, the adverse elements, and the gods: but I haste to prevent his speed. Executioner, do your office."

As he closed, a voice in the distance cried, "Stop the execution!" which was repeated by the whole assembly. A man rode up at full speed, mounted the scaffold, and embraced Pythias, crying, "You are safe, my beloved friend! I now have nothing but death to suffer, and am delivered from reproaches for having endangered a life so much dearer than my own."

Pythias replied, "Fatal haste, cruel impatience! What envious powers have wrought impossibilities in your favor? But I will not be wholly disappointed. Since I cannot die to save, I will not survive you."

The king heard, and was moved to tears. Ascending the scaffold he cried, "Live, live, ye incomparable pair! Ye have borne unquestionable testimony to the existence of virtue; and that virtue equally evinces the existence of a God to reward it. Live happy, live renowned, and oh! form me by your precepts, as ye have invited me by your example, to be worthy of the participation of so sacred a friendship."

If heathenism had such friendships, what may be expected of Christianity?[11]

What does the world see in your friendships? How is Christ reflected in them? And what are you doing to extend Christian friendship to people who don't yet know the Lord? We have a chance to be a witness for Jesus Christ through our friendships with believers and nonbelievers alike.

> *Father God, thank You for the friends I have who will, like Onesiphorus did for Paul, stand beside me in all situations. These friends are always by my side when I need them. And, God, teach me to be the kind of friend that Onesiphorus was to Paul. Help me be alert to the needs of people in my life, and then use me to help with those needs. I praise You for giving me opportunities to be a friend. Amen.*

Taking Action

- Who needs you to be his Onesiphorus today? What will you do to refresh and encourage him?

- Get in touch with a friend you haven't seen for a while.

- Let a friend know how much you value him.

Reading On

Proverbs 18:24   Luke 10:30-37

Your Most Important Decision

SCRIPTURE READING: Joshua 24:14-15

KEY VERSE: Joshua 24:15

*[Joshua said,] "As for me and my household,
we will serve the LORD."*

Some decisions we make in life have eternal consequences, and choosing whom to worship is one such decision. Thousands of years ago, Joshua faced the same decision you and I face. Which god will we worship? Will we—and our families with us—follow the gods of the world or the one true God?

Joshua was a man of courage, strength, determination, and faith. He was a leader in his family and in his nation. And as related in today's Scripture reading, this man of God reminds us that we worship the gods we want to. And then he boldly announces that he and his family will serve the Lord.

Which gods are you serving? Poor choices in the past may be affecting how you answer that question today. If you're tired of being a slave to poor decisions of the past, please know that you can have freedom in Christ. You can commit your life to Jesus and let Him turn it around.

Paul wrote, "If you declare with your mouth, 'Jesus is Lord,' and believe in your heart that God raised him from the dead, you will be saved. For it is with your heart that you believe and are justified, and it is with your mouth that you profess your faith and are saved" (Romans 10:9-10). In light of this promise, will you make a decision for Christ today? It will be the best decision of your life! Don't delay. Don't wait until it's too late.

Three times a soldier in a hospital picked up a tract containing the hymn "Will You Go?" Twice he threw it down. The third time, however, he read it, thought about it, and, taking his pencil, wrote deliberately in the margin these words: "By the grace of God, I will try to go, John Waugh, Company G, Tenth Regiment, P.R.V.C." That night, he went to a prayer meeting, read aloud his resolution, requested prayers for his salvation, and said, "I am not ashamed of Christ now; but I am ashamed of myself for having been so long ashamed of Him." He was killed a few months later. How timely was his resolution!

Decide now for the first time—or reconfirm an earlier decision—that you and your family will serve the Lord.

> *Father God, each day I choose what god I will worship. Just as Joshua did, I choose You, Jehovah God. I want to serve You with all my heart and soul. Please renew that desire in me on a daily basis and help me lead my family to You. I love You. Amen.*

Taking Action

- Read Romans 8:1 and 1 John 1:9.

- Decide to serve the Lord or recommit to serving Him. Write today's date in your journal or on the first inside page of your Bible. Also write Romans 8:1 and 1 John 1:9 down for later reference.

- Tell a friend of your decision. Ask him to pray for your spiritual growth and to hold you accountable to serving God and God alone.

Reading On

Romans 3:23   Acts 16:30-31

Romans 6:23   Ephesians 2:8-9

Reining Your Tongue

Scripture reading: James 1:19-27

Key verse: James 1:26

*Those who consider themselves religious and yet
do not keep a tight rein on their tongues
deceives themselves, and their religion is worthless.*

In *All I Really Need to Know I Learned in Kindergarten,* Robert Fulghum proposes that in this noisy world of ours it's important to have a quiet spirit. He tells of villagers in the Solomon Islands who felled a tree by screaming at it for 30 days. The tree died, confirming the Islanders's theory that hollering kills a living thing's spirit. Fulghum then considers the things that he and his neighbors yell at—the wife, the kids, the telephone, the lawn mower that won't start, traffic, umpires, machines. He offers this observation:

> Don't know what good it does. Machines and things just
> sit there. Even kicking doesn't always help. As for people,
> well, the Solomon Islanders may have a point. Yelling at
> living things does tend to kill the spirit in them. Sticks
> and stones may break our bones, but words will break
> our hearts.[12]

If we could only remember this each time we want to yell. Too often, we try to get control over a person or situation by raising our voices. But that is just the opposite of what we need to do. Try lowering your voice next time you're tempted to raise it. See what happens.

The world is full of people dead in spirit because someone didn't realize that loud voices can kill. Try dealing with the situations of life more quietly. Rein your tongue. Let it speak words that arise from a peaceful spirit.

Father God, my speech is a constant reminder that I, like Paul, do what I don't want to do and don't do what I want to do. You know how I struggle and fail to control my tongue. Forgive me for the hurts I've caused and heal the hurts in others. Lord, be at work transforming me so that I can rein my tongue. Amen.

Taking Action

- Take some time right now to evaluate how you use your words and your voice in your life. Note those areas where you want to change, and write out a specific step for each one so you will do it.

- Today practice lowering your voice when you feel like raising it.

- Either in person, by phone, by email, or in a letter, apologize to someone to whom you've talked too harshly.

Reading On

Ephesians 4:29   Matthew 7:15-20

John 15:1-9

"I'm Special Because..."

SCRIPTURE READING: Psalm 139:13-17

KEY VERSE: Psalm 139:14
*I praise you because I am fearfully and
wonderfully made; your works are wonderful,
I know that full well.*

Whenever the grandchildren come over, Emilie honors someone at the table with our red plate that says, "You Are Special." Years ago, when Emilie asked our seven-year-old grandson Chad, "Who should get the plate today?" we weren't surprised when he said, "How about me?"

After we sat down at the table and said the blessing, Chad spoke up. "I think it would be very nice if everyone around the table told me why they think I'm special." We got a chuckle out of that, but we also thought it was a good idea. After we told Chad why we thought he was special, Chad said, "Now I want to tell you why I think I'm special. I'm special because I'm a child of God."

Chad was absolutely right. Psalm 139:13-14 tells us that God knew each of us *before* we were born. He knit us together in our mothers' wombs, and we are "wonderfully made." Each of us can confidently say "I'm valuable because I am a child of God!"

Verse 16 of this psalm says, "All the days ordained for me were written in your book before one of them came to be." It's not by accident that you are reading this selection today! God wants you to know how valuable you are. He has given you unique qualities, talents, and gifts. You are His child, created by Him. He loves you more than any earthly father could, and He cares for you even when you feel worthless and far away from Him. His love for you, His one-of-a-kind child, will never fail.

> *Father God, thank You for making me the person I am and for putting within me a heart to love You more and more each day. Help me today to draw nearer to You. As I go about my day, I know that I will never be alone. Thank You for always being with me. Amen.*

Taking Action

- Thank God for who you are, His special child.

- Today honor someone in your family for being special. A special plate isn't necessary. Be creative and come up with your own way of designating who's special.

- At an upcoming family meal, talk about why each person is special to each family member and to God.

- Kidnap one of your children for lunch this week. Find out the exact time school breaks for lunch, notify the school office, and show up outside the classroom door. A nearby fast-food restaurant will do the trick and make your child feel special indeed.

Reading On

Psalm 73:28   Ephesians 1:4

Questions and Answers for Life

SCRIPTURE READING: Romans 8:28-39

KEY VERSE: Romans 8:28
*We know that in all things God works for the good
of those who love him, who have been called
according to his purpose.*

I n today's Scripture passage, the apostle Paul asks and answers
some key questions for life. Take a look at the powerful truths he
outlines in Romans 8.

1. "What, then, shall we say in response to these things?" (verse
31). Paul has written that God

- foreknew us
- predestined us to be conformed to the likeness of His
  Son
- called us
- justified us
- glorified us

Then comes the question—"What, then, shall we say in response
to these things?" Each one of us answers that question by how we
live.

2. "If God is for us, who can be against us?" (verse 31).

Answer: Nothing—absolutely nothing on earth or in heaven

above—can work against us because the Lord of the universe is for us. We have everything in God through His Son Jesus.

3. "He who did not spare his own Son, but gave him up for us all—how will he not also, along with him, graciously give us all things?" (verse 32).

Answer: God will graciously give us all the things that we need according to His will for our lives. What an assurance to know that what we have has passed through the Father's hands.

4. "Who will bring any charge against those whom God has chosen?" (verse 33).

Answer: No one—absolutely no one.

5. "Who then is the one who condemns?" (verse 34).

Answer: No one can condemn us because God, who is on our side, has justified us. Furthermore, Jesus Christ sits at the right hand of God interceding for us.

6. "Who shall separate us from the love of Christ?" (verse 35).

Answer: No one! And Paul gets specific. "Neither death nor life, neither angels nor demons, neither the present nor the future, nor any powers, neither height nor depth, nor anything else in all creation, will be able to separate us from the love of God that is in Christ Jesus our Lord" (verses 38-39).

Turn to these questions Paul asks and the answers he gives when the world crowds in and you're feeling alone. In His holy Word, God answers questions like the ones Paul asked, as well as any questions you might ask—and Scripture's answers are the only reliable ones. So during tough times, keep in mind that "in all things God works for the good of those who love him, who have been called according to his purpose" (Romans 8:28).

Father God, when questions arise, guide me to the answers in Your Word. Give me discernment to ask the right questions and wisdom to discover Your answers. And thank You that even when I blow it by asking the wrong questions or listening to the wrong answers, You can work my mistakes for my good. Amen.

Taking Action

- What did you learn from today's Scripture reading that you didn't know before?

- What question for life do you want answered? Write it down and then go to Scripture and talk to God. Also, don't hesitate to talk with a pastor, Bible-study leader, or mature Christian for help in finding the answer.

Reading On

2 Timothy 3:16   1 John 1:5–2:2

Philippians 4:13

The Way Up

SCRIPTURE READING: 1 Peter 5:5-11

KEY VERSE: 1 Peter 5:5

All of you, clothe yourselves with humility toward one another, because, "God opposes the proud but gives grace to the humble."

Think about the last touchdown you saw scored. How did the player who carried the ball into the end zone react? Did he throw the ball to the ground as hard as he could? Do a jig? Give big bear hugs? Whatever he did, my guess is he didn't show much humility. And football players aren't the only ones short of humility. Baseball, basketball, and tennis players haven't mastered humility either, and that's not surprising in our world, which has gone mad with pride.

I believe, however, that humility is key to successful relationships, but humility is a slippery characteristic. Once you think of yourself as humble—you're not! So people who are genuinely humble never perceive themselves as humble. Despite humility's slippery nature, the apostle Peter wrote today's Scripture verse and then continued with, "Humble yourselves, therefore, under God's mighty hand, that he may lift you up in due time" (1 Peter 5:6).

Peter's words sharply contradict the talk about climbing the corporate ladder, upward mobility, self-assertion, and winning through intimidation. Some people focus on moving up, but God's focus is different. The way up with God is always down. Peter's exhortation to be "clothed with humility" is a *command*, not a suggestion. And note that "*God opposes the proud.*" The moment we allow pride in our hearts, the resistance of God begins. We also learn that "the LORD detests all the proud of heart" and "pride brings a person low" (Proverbs 16:5; 29:23).

Against that backdrop, hear again the truth that Peter teaches. When you are clothed with humility, God ends His resistance against you. When we are humble, God promises to exalt us at the proper time.

- "Humility comes before honor" (Proverbs 15:33).
- "Humble yourselves before the Lord, and he will lift you up" (James 4:10).
- "He has brought down rulers from their thrones but has lifted up the humble" (Luke 1:52).

But what exactly is humility?

- It is moral realism, the result of a fresh revelation of God.
- It is esteeming others.
- It is a fruit of repentance.
- It is the attitude that rejoices in the success of others.
- It is freedom from having to be right.
- It is a foundation of unity.
- It is a mark of authenticity.
- It is a fruit of brokenness.
- It is a quality that catches the attention of God.

Our only response to God's holiness is humility, and the end result of our humility is holiness. As we kneel as servants at the feet of our Lord, ready and willing to serve Him and His people, He will lift us up.

Father God, give me such a clear vision of You in all Your majesty and holiness that I am humbled. Please make me aware of any false pride in my life. Send me a friend who can help me be accountable in this area of my life. And may the humility that comes from truly knowing You characterize all that I say and do. Amen.

Taking Action

■ List three or four areas of your life (business, athletics, cars, income, talents, and so forth) that tend to make you prideful. Think about how you can embrace humility in each of these areas.

■ Why do you think pride ruins relationships? Jot down a few thoughts.

Reading On

Proverbs 22:4   Philippians 2:8

Psalm 45:3-4   1 Peter 2:21

The Master Potter

Scripture reading: Jeremiah 18:2-6

Key verse: Jeremiah 18:6
"Can I not do with you, Israel, as this potter does?"
declares the Lord.

When our son, Brad, was in elementary school, his teacher asked the class to shape clay into something. Molded and shaped with his small hands, this red dinosaur-type thing that Brad proudly brought home is still on our bookshelf today. Later, in high school, Brad enrolled in a ceramics class. His first pieces were crooked and misshaped, but as time went on he made some pieces of real art—vases, pots, pitchers, and various other kinds of pottery. Many pieces of clay he threw on the wheel would take a different direction than he'd intended. Brad would work and work to reshape the clay, and sometimes he would have to start all over, working and working to make it was exactly the way he wanted it to be.

With each one of us, God has taken a handful of clay to make us exactly who He wants us to be. He is the Master Potter, and we are the vessels in His house. As He shapes us on the potter's wheel, He works on the inside and the outside. He essentially says, "I am with you. I am the Lord of your life, and I will build within you a strong foundation based upon my Word."

The Master Potter also uses the circumstances of life to shape us into who He wants us to be. When a child dies, a job loss occurs, fire destroys a home, finances dissolve, a marriage falls apart, or the children rebel, the Potter can seem very far away. We may feel forgotten by God, and we might pull away from Him because we think He's let us down. As time passes, He seems even more distant, and it seems that the Potter's work is put on hold. But God said, "Never will I leave you; never will I forsake you" (Hebrews 13:5).

When we feel far from God, we need to remember that He didn't put us on the shelf. We are the ones who moved away. He's ready to continue working to mold us into the people He created us to be.

We also need to remember that in pottery the hot temperatures set the clay so the vessel is strong and, if applicable, doesn't leak. The true beauty of the clay and glaze comes out only after the firing. The fires of life can do the same for our faith and our character, and we can rest in the knowledge that the Master Potter is at work.

Father God, You know I feel distant from You at times, but I know I'm the one who moved. I've been trying to be the captain of my ship, but it's not working. I want to get back on course through Your navigation. Shape me into the person You designed me to be. I want to work with You and be malleable in Your hands. Amen.

Taking Action

- When have you withdrawn from God or felt forgotten by Him? What circumstances prompted those feelings?

- What will you do to become more aware of the Master Potter—His love for you, His plans for you, and His ongoing work in your life?

Reading On

Psalm 73:26	Hebrews 13:5
Psalm 121:7	Romans 12:2

"[Lord,] those who love Your law have great peace,
and nothing causes them to stumble."

Psalm 119:165 NASB

Using Your Talents

SCRIPTURE READING: Matthew 25:14-30

KEY VERSE: Matthew 25:21
Well done, good and faithful servant!

God calls us to faithfully use our talents for Him, and He warns those who do not use the talents He has given them. Now consider what God is saying specifically to you in this parable Jesus told.

What talents has God given you? Too often we think of talents as fully developed abilities, but it is only as we cultivate our talents that they become mature. Furthermore, we must be willing to take the risk of using our talents. When we do, we find out how far God can take us.

Let's look at the parable told in today's Scripture reading. The first two servants were willing to take a risk. They received a 100-percent return for their efforts, and their master said to each one, "Well done, good and faithful servant! You have been faithful with a few things; I will put you in charge of many things. Come and share your master's happiness!" (verses 21 and 23). Note that despite their different talents and abilities, the first two servants received the same reward, indicating that God requires us to be faithful in the use of our abilities, whatever they are.

If you want to be successful in God's eyes, you must first be faithful with a few things. Then God will put you in charge of many things. Is there a talent that people keep saying you're good at, but you just shrug it off as not being good enough? Do you think no one could be blessed by your talent? This passage tells you to take the risk. Volunteer for that position, write that book, sign up for that class, offer to help with that project. Listen to God today as He calls you to the life of adventure that comes with using the gifts He's given you. Don't limit God.

Now let's look at the warning to those of us who don't use our talents. The third servant was afraid. Unwilling to take a risk with the one talent his master gave him, he went and buried it in the ground. Are you burying your talents? God will hold you responsible for what you do with your talents and with your life. This third servant is condemned for his sloth and indifference.

God wants you to take the risk of using the talents He's given you, even if they don't seem like much to you. Take the first step today, and you'll be amazed at what God can do! And you'll also be blessed when one day you stand before God and hear Him say, "Well done, good and faithful servant!"

> *Father God, at times I don't feel I have any talents, but I know You've given each of Your children special gifts. Today I'm asking You for direction. How do You want me to use my talents for Your glory? Thank You for listening to my prayer. Help me hear Your answer. Amen.*

Taking Action

- Ask God today to reveal to you those special gifts that He wants you to develop.

- Ask a friend to share with you his perception of your special gifts or talents.

- Develop a plan and a timetable to begin using these talents and gifts for the Lord.

Reading On

Exodus 4:10-12   Ephesians 3:14-21

"Teach us to number our days,
that we may gain a heart of wisdom."

Psalm 90:12

Stewardship at Home

SCRIPTURE READING: Psalm 127:1–128:4

KEY VERSE: Psalm 127:3
*Children are a heritage from the LORD,
offspring a reward from him.*

In a recent Bible study Emilie attended, the teacher asked the women, "Did you feel loved by your parents when you were a child?" The answers were disturbing and, for the parents, quite convicting:

- "They were too busy for me."
- "I spent too much time with the babysitters."
- "Dad took us on trips, but he played golf all the time we were away."
- "I got in their way. I wasn't important to them."
- "Mom was too involved at the country club to spend time with us."
- "Mom didn't have to work, but she did so she wouldn't have to be home with us children."
- "A lot of pizzas were delivered to our house on Friday nights when my parents went out for the evening."

What do you think your children would say if someone asked them, "Do you feel loved by your parents?" Which of your actions would support their answer, positive or negative?

Today's Scripture reading gives us some principles for building a family in which children are confident that their parents love them. First, the psalmist addresses the foundation and protection of the home: "Unless the LORD builds the house, the builders labor in vain. Unless the LORD watches over the city, the guards stand watch in vain" (Psalm 127:1). Walls were built around cities for protection. They could be up to 40 feet tall and wide enough to race chariots on. The people of the Old Testament knew they needed protection from the enemy, but they were also smart enough to know that walls could be climbed over, knocked down, or broken apart. They realized that their ultimate security was the Lord standing guard over the city.

Are you looking to God to help you build your home? Are you trusting the Lord to be the guard over your family? Many forces in today's world threaten the family. When I drive the Southern California freeways, I see parents who are burning the candle at both ends to provide all the material things they think will make their families happy. We rise early and retire late. Psalm 127:2 tells us that these efforts are futile: "In vain you rise early and stay up late, toiling for food to eat—for he grants sleep to those he loves." We are to do our best to provide for and protect our families, but we must trust in God first and foremost to take care of them.

Then, in verse 3 (NASB), we read that "children are a gift of the LORD." In Hebrew, the language the Old Testament was written in, "gift" means "property" or "possession." Truly, God has loaned us our children to care for and to enjoy for a certain period of time, but they remain His property, His possessions. As stewards of our children, we are to take care of them. And that takes time.

I love to grow vegetables each summer, and I'm always amazed at what it takes to get a good crop. I have to cultivate the soil, sow the seeds, water, fertilize, weed, and prune. Raising children takes a lot of time, care, nurturing, and cultivating too. We can't neglect these responsibilities if we're going to produce good fruit. Left to themselves, our children—like gardens—will quickly become overgrown with weeds. When I do tend the garden, however, I'm rewarded by corn, tomatoes, cucumbers, and beans. Just as the harvest is my reward, so God-fearing children are their parents' reward.

Next, comparing children to arrows in the hands of a warrior, Psalm 127:4-5 talks about how parents are to handle their offspring. Wise and skillful parents will know their children, understand them, and carefully point them in the right direction before shooting them into the world. And, as I learned in a college archery class, shooting an arrow straight and hitting a target is a lot harder in real life than it looks like in the movies or on television. (I sure wasn't Robin Hood!) Likewise, godly and skillful parenting isn't easy.

The last section of today's selection teaches the importance of the Lord's presence in the home.

- The Lord is central to a home's happiness (Psalm 128:1-2).

- A wife who knows the Lord will be a source of beauty and life in the home (verse 3).

- With the Lord's blessing, children will flourish like olive trees, which generously provide food, oil, and shelter (verse 3).

What can you do to make the Lord's presence more recognizable in your home? What kind of steward are you being in your home? God has entrusted to you some very special people—your children. You will be held accountable for how you take care of them. But you're not in it alone. God offers guidelines, like those we looked at today, plus His wisdom and His love to help you do the job and do it well.

Father God, forgive me for the ways I shortchange my kids. Help me know how to slow down the pace of life. Remind me to stay very aware that my children will only be with me for just a short time, and that how I treat them will affect them and their children's lives too. Continue to teach me how to be the father You want me to be. Amen.

Taking Action

- "Our attitude toward our children reveals our attitude toward God." What does this statement mean to you?

- When you're talking to your children today, make a point of looking right into their eyes as you listen.

- Where do you need to be more consistent in teaching your children what is right and what is wrong?

- Give your child the gift of time—today and every day.

- Have you ever camped out inside? This weekend, go camping in your family room. Get your sleeping bags and a flashlight. Make shadow animals on the walls and ceilings. Don't forget the popcorn and hot chocolate.

- Review your calendar and plan ahead to do something with your kids.

Reading On

James 1:19-20   Proverbs 18:10

Matthew 18:5-6   Proverbs 16:24

"Do not call to mind the former things, or ponder things of the past. Behold, I will do something new."

Isaiah 43:18-19 NASB

A Treasure in Jars of Clay

SCRIPTURE READINGS: 2 Corinthians 4:7; 6:3-10

KEY VERSE: 2 Corinthians 4:7
*We have this treasure in jars of clay to show that this
all-surpassing power is from God and not from us.*

In today's Scripture, we read that we are "jars of clay," and we hold the great treasure of the gospel within. Isn't it interesting that you and I hide our treasures in vaults and safe deposit boxes, but God trusts His treasure to common clay pots? The only value our clay pot has is from the treasure inside.

I'm continually amazed that God can and does use me, an ordinary person who is willing to be used for Christ's sake. Simply stated, Christianity is Jesus Christ. He is the treasure residing in the Christian. And God trusts us—even commands us—to share that treasure with other people.

Do you honestly believe that God can use you, a clay pot with a great treasure inside, to do the work He has called you to do for His kingdom? If we men will believe and act on this promise, God's kingdom will reign more fully in our hearts, our homes, our churches, our cities, our country, and the world.

Father God, don't let me hide my treasure—the knowledge of Your Son and my Savior Jesus Christ—in this clay pot. I want the people around me to see what a precious and valuable treasure I possess by Your grace. And, Lord, I am only a clay pot, but in Your hands and strengthened by Your all-surpassing power, You can use me for Your kingdom. I pray that You will do so. Amen.

Taking Action

- What current problems make you feel like a clay pot?

- Where in your life do you think God wants to use you for His kingdom?

- Make these two lists the focus of your prayers. Know that God will give you the strength you need to deal with life's challenges. Know too that He wants to use you for His kingdom. As you pray, be ready for Him to work in and through your life.

Reading On

Matthew 10:28-29   Philippians 4:13

Your Wife, Your Friend

SCRIPTURE READING: Genesis 2:18-23

KEY VERSE: Genesis 2:18

*The LORD God said, "It is not good
for the man to be alone.
I will make a helper suitable for him."*

In Genesis 2:18-23, we see that when God created the first woman (and wife), He also created the first friend. A wife is indeed to be her husband's friend. Emilie has certainly been mine. And, as today's passage shows, that's what God intends for married couples. Let's look more closely at these Scriptures.

- God gives the woman to the man to be "a helper suitable for him" (Genesis 2:18). How is your wife your helper? How does she help your work? Your time at home? Does she often seem to know what you need or want before you ask? How often do you let her know you appreciate her helpfulness?

- God creates woman from man's rib (verses 21-22). In Genesis 1:27, we learn that God created human beings in His image. The fact that each of us is created in God's image calls us to honor and respect one another. What do you do to show your wife that you honor and respect her? How do you show and tell your wife that you love her?

- Adam perceived Eve as part of his own bone and own

flesh (2:23). If I recognize that Emilie is actually part of me, I will want to treat her as well as I treat myself. I will want to take good care of her and provide for her every need. What selfish behavior do you need to apologize for and change? What could you do to take better care of your wife?

In light of what you've seen in Scripture, consider the following definition of a friend:

> And what is a friend? Many things…A friend is someone you are comfortable with, someone whose company you prefer. A friend is someone you can count on—not only for support, but for honesty.
>
> A friend is one who believes in you…someone with whom you can share your dreams. In fact, a real friend is a person you want to share all of life with—and the sharing doubles the fun.
>
> When you are hurting and you can share your struggle with a friend, it eases the pain. A friend offers you safety and trust…Whatever you say will never be used against you.
>
> A friend will laugh with you, but not at you…A friend will pray with you…and for you.
>
> My friend is one who hears my cry of pain, who senses my struggle, who shares my lows as well as my highs.[13]

In such a friendship, nothing is hidden. It's built on trust, and this takes time to grow and develop. What better context for this kind of friendship to grow than in your marriage? How does your marriage measure up?

Father God, I want to be a friend to my wife. Help me understand her better so that I will know how to support, encourage, and love her. Give me patience and a humble spirit that is willing to serve, to forgive, and to ask for forgiveness. Amen.

Taking Action

- Do something with your wife that you don't normally like to do, such as watch a romantic movie, take her shopping, or plan a special dinner.

- Buy your wife a card or write her a note telling her how much you enjoy having her as a friend.

Reading On

Proverbs 18:24   Amos 3:3

Ecclesiastes 4:9

"Let no unwholesome word proceed from your mouth, but only such a word as is good for edification...so that it will give grace to those who hear."

Ephesians 4:29 NASB

The Guy Who Drew the Line

SCRIPTURE READING: Ephesians 1:3-14

KEY VERSE: Ephesians 1:4
*[God] chose us in him before the creation
of the world to be holy and blameless in his sight.*

The judge looked down from the bench and, in a somber voice, declared, "Mr. Wilson, this is your day of reckoning!" Then he sentenced him to seven and one-half years in federal prison.

In response, Wilson's lawyer requested that he be allowed a few minutes with his family and friends before surrendering to the authorities.

The judge replied, "Mr. Wilson is going to be taken by the marshals right now. You should have thought of that before."

Wilson was one of four California men convicted of financial fraud and sentenced to prison in this particular case. Five men were originally investigated, but the fifth, Mark Jacobs, was not arrested and charged.

Jacobs had been invited to join the financial scheme by four friends (the men sent to jail) in a weekly Bible study. They had assured him their plan was totally legal. Yet something inside him said it wasn't right. While it was hard to say no to good friends, he chose to go with his conscience and tell them he wouldn't participate.

The lawyers for the four convicted men pleaded with the judge that their clients had simply made mistakes of poor judgment. They were good men who loved their wives and kids, gave to charities, and were active in their churches. The crime involved a gray area, crossing a line that wasn't clear.

The judge disagreed. "It is not hard to determine where the line is," he said. "The guy who drew the line is Mark Jacobs. He knew what was right and what was wrong, and he didn't hesitate. Hopefully, now we will have fewer people who are willing to walk up to the line and dabble with going over the line. We will have people like Mr. Jacobs, who wouldn't touch this thing with a ten-foot pole."[14]

Too often in America today, men in responsible positions don't know where to draw the line. We see it in the worlds of high finance, religion, politics, entertainment, and sports. Our ethics and morality are no longer firmly anchored in the Judeo-Christian principles of our forefathers. Without these guidelines to show us where to draw the line, we are confused and adrift when it comes to knowing right and wrong. We aren't able to live the kind of life Christ calls us to live.

In 1 Peter 1:6-7, we are reminded that we become pure just as gold does. It's a process. As one writer explains, "Gold has to be heated and reheated and reheated several times for the alloys and impurities to be brought to the surface, where the goldsmith can remove them. If you forget that becoming pure is a process, you risk becoming overwhelmed by discouragement when you experience those inevitable setbacks."[15]

Wanting to be pure in a world of gray isn't enough. You have to develop a plan of action if you are to become more like Jesus. In "Black-and-White Living in a Gray World," Dr. Gary Oliver lists some simple steps you and I can take so that God can move us beyond good intentions and down the path toward purity:

1. Make a decision (Daniel 1:8).

2. Choose to put first things first (Mark 7:15,20-23).

3. Determine where the line is and then stay a safe distance behind it (James 1:14-15).

4. Guard your heart (Matthew 6:21).

5. Guard your mind (Colossians 3:2).

6. Guard your eyes (Job 31:1).

7. Guard the little things (Luke 16:10).[16]

These steps are simply stated, but not necessarily easy to live out. I challenge you to try. Ask God to strengthen your commitment to Him and to guide your thoughts as you turn to Him to learn how to be a godly and pure man, a man who knows where to draw the line in our confusing world.

Father God, I come before You concerned about how I can live a pure life. I want to make right decisions. I want to live a life that reflects to my family and to the world that I am a child of Yours. When I need to make choices in this confusing world but don't know where Your line is, please take a stick and draw that line so I can see it. Give me a daily hunger for Your Word so I will learn and live according to the principles You teach there. Help me be a guy who draws the line where You do. Amen.

Taking Action

■ Develop a specific plan based on the seven steps just outlined that will help you live a purer, more Christlike life.

■ Read your Bible daily. Start with the Gospel of John, the

book of Psalms, or the book of Proverbs. As you read, ask yourself what God is showing you about how to live a pure life.

▪ Find a friend who will hold you accountable to your plan or, better yet, join you in your study.

Reading On

Matthew 5:8   Ephesians 4:1

Ephesians 5:1

"Do not withhold your mercy from me, LORD; may your love and your truth always protect me."

Psalm 40:11

For the Traveling Man

- Decide beforehand not to indulge in pornography. Most mistakes are made when you haven't resolved to avoid the material before you leave home.

- Whenever possible, stay with friends when you're traveling alone. If you're around others, you're less likely to give in to temptations.

- When you check in at a hotel, request that the staff block the adult movies from your room. If you do, you'll face much less temptation later in the evening.

- Develop a game plan for your evening. Outline the specific things you want to see and do before settling in for the night. If you fill your time with productive uses, you'll be less tempted.

- Make a habit of reading Scripture before turning on the television. Try Psalm 101:2-4; Romans 12:21; 1 Corinthians 6:18-20; Ephesians 6:10-17; James 4:17.[17]

A House Divided

SCRIPTURE READING: Mark 3:24-27

KEY VERSE: Mark 3:25
*If a house is divided against itself,
that house cannot stand.*

A house divided against itself cannot stand," Abraham Lincoln said when he accepted the nomination for a United States Senate seat. "Either the opponents of slavery will arrest the further spread of it and place it where the public mind shall rest in the belief that it is in the course of ultimate extinction, or its advocates will push it forward, till it shall become alike lawful in all the states, old as well as new—north as well as south."

Lincoln's stand against slavery and for the equality of peoples resulted in his defeat in the election, but he responded philosophically: "Though I now sink out of view and shall be forgotten, I believe I have made some marks which will tell for the cause of civil liberty long after I am gone." Well, Lincoln certainly didn't "sink out of view"! Later, as president of the United States, he worked to bring together those who had been at war and to heal the hurts that had divided the nation and even some families within it.

Many families today are divided and need to be brought together; many hurts in those families need to be healed. I've watched this happen in Emilie's family. Her two aunts were sisters who hadn't spoken to each other for ten years. The initial disagreement, as slight as it may have been, became unbridgeable. Neither would apologize or admit to being wrong. Having watched this go on for a long time, Emilie decided that she was going to be the peacemaker. She arranged a family gathering and invited both aunts. After just a short time, the two began to open up and talk to each other. By the end of the evening, they had made amends. They were able to enjoy the last 15 years of their lives together.

Maybe such division exists in your family. If so, know that the warning in today's Scripture is for you—"If a kingdom is divided against itself, that kingdom cannot stand." If a family remains divided, it will collapse. What can you do to help bring unity to your family? What can you do to help healing come to your home? Whatever steps you decide to take, know that you'll need much patience and many prayers. As you seek God's blessing on your attempts to rebuild your home, ask Him to give you wisdom and understanding. Know too that it will take time to rebuild what has been destroyed by division; don't feel that it must be resolved quickly. Be willing to walk by faith, not by sight, and pray earnestly for healing each step of the way.

Father God, use me to be a healer in my family. Allow me to help bring unity where there is now division. Show me the steps to take. I thank You that You will be with me and my family members as we build bridges and learn to forgive one another. Amen.

Taking Action

- Where in your family is there division? Where is there a need for healing and reunification?

- What one person could you start focusing your prayers on?

- Ask your wife to join you in praying about this person and the goal of unity within the family.

- Develop a plan for reuniting this family member with the

family, and then take the risky step of putting that plan into action.

Reading On

Matthew 12:25-27   Luke 11:17-22

"I am confident of this very thing,
that He who began a good work in you
will perfect it until the day of Christ Jesus."

Philippians 1:6 NASB

What Do Women Do All Day?

SCRIPTURE READING: Proverbs 31:10-31

KEY VERSES: Proverbs 31:10-11

*A wife of noble character who can find? She is worth
far more than rubies. Her husband has full confidence
in her and lacks nothing of value.*

Do you ever wonder what your wife is doing all day while you're
at work? If you're the chief or only breadwinner, you might
think, *What my wife does is important—but it's not like what I do!*
But simply looking around your own home can open your eyes to
the demands of home and family management.

As I've watched my wife, Emilie, and many of her friends, I've
been amazed at how much they get done—all at once. They seem
able to juggle a lot more at one time than I can. I remember when
the children were younger and I was home for a few days—I couldn't
wait to get back to work! In fact, on several occasions I checked
myself out of the house before the doctor gave me a release. Why? I
couldn't handle so much going on at one time.

If watching your wife in action doesn't give you reason enough to
appreciate her, consider the standards God has for your wife. These
are listed in today's passage:

- She is very valuable (verse 10).

- We are to have full confidence in her (verse 11).

- Our wife is to bring us good, not harm (verse 12).

- She is to be industrious (verse 13).

- She is to be a good cook, shopper, delegator, Realtor, gardener, overseer, seamstress; she works long hours; she is to be compassionate and serene (verses 14-22).

- She is to bring respect and honor to her husband (verse 23).

- She is to have a good sense of humor, be wise with her words, and not be lazy (verses 24-27).

- She is to be respected and praised by her children (verse 28).

- She is to be praised by her husband (verses 28-29).

- She has no comparison in all the world (verse 29).

- She is to major on the majors, not the minors (verse 30).

- She is to be rewarded and praised (verse 31).

That's a tall order for your wife and mine! A wife who strives to meet these standards is a real helpmate. God knows what we need in order for us to function properly as a husband and the head of the family, and He tells us here. Our response to this gift of a godly and hardworking wife is to appreciate her and thank God for her! Take time today to consider all that your wife does all day—and then let her know you appreciate her.

> *Father God, thank You for reminding me today of all that my wife does for our family. Forgive me for the times I take her for granted and take for granted her contributions to our home. Teach me to encourage her and show her how much I appreciate her. She is definitely worthy of praise. Amen.*

Taking Action

- Include in a special "I love you" or "thank-you" card some fun confetti in the shapes of hearts, dogs, cats, stars, moons, and so forth.

- Take your wife shopping this evening and buy her a new outfit.

- Be a genie by granting your wife three wishes.

- Tell your wife that you are thankful for her because... (list as many reasons as possible).

- You do, of course, have a picnic basket in your car trunk at all times, don't you?

- Just thought you might like to know—the proper way to kiss a woman's hand is to hold her hand gently but firmly in a comfortable position. Lower your lips to her hand. Do not raise her hand to your lips.

Reading On

Proverbs 12:4   1 Peter 3:1-6

"Woman is the glory of man."

1 Corinthians 11:7

The Los Angeles Marathon

SCRIPTURE READING: Hebrews 12:1-12

KEY VERSES: Hebrews 12:1-2

Since we are surrounded by such a great cloud of witnesses, let us throw off everything that hinders and the sin that so easily entangles. And let us run with perseverance the race marked out for us, fixing our eyes on Jesus, the pioneer and perfecter of faith. For the joy set before him he endured the cross, scorning its shame, and sat down at the right hand of the throne of God.

Our son, Brad, has always been an athlete. Name the sport, and he could do it—and do it well. In high school he played football. In college he played volleyball and tennis. After graduation he and some college friends began doing triathlons (swimming, biking, and running), and Brad did very well. In the spring of 1991, Brad entered the Los Angeles Marathon. He worked out hard and long to prepare for the 26.2 mile run. Every day before or after work, he ran between 6 and 19 miles, enough to total 75 miles a week. Finally, the day of the marathon arrived. At the sound of the gun, over 20,000 runners were off, including Brad.

That day wasn't a good day for my son. Although he'd prepared for months and faithfully maintained a rigorous training schedule, he hit the wall by the tenth mile. Physically, he was Mr. America, but that day he just wasn't able to perform. He continued to run, struggling painfully on. Brad finished the race—he always finishes whatever he starts—but his time was 3 hours and 50 minutes. His goal had been just a little over three hours.

As tough a day as it was for Brad, he helped me appreciate the truth of today's text in Hebrews. In this race called life, we are to keep our eyes on Jesus and continue running toward the mark He has set for us. We must discipline ourselves to study God's Word and get to know Him better so that we can continue on even when we hit the wall. When we do, He produces in our hearts a harvest of righteousness and peace. We become mature, strong, and able to help others through their struggles. And when we struggle and even fall along the way, we need to do what Brad did. Rather than looking back at a bad race and asking why, he looks ahead to the day when he'll run it again.

The author of the book of Hebrews tells us other things about this race of life:

- We are surrounded by other Christians and can get support from them.
- We need to throw off everything that hinders us.
- We need to throw off the sin that entangles us.
- We need to run with perseverance and determination.
- And we need to fix our eyes on Jesus, the pioneer and perfecter of our faith.
- With God's help, we'll run this race and cross the finish line in His perfect time.

Father God, help me each day to run with perseverance the race of life so that I will bring glory to Your name. Teach me self-discipline. Give me Your strength to go the distance. Amen.

Taking Action

■ List those areas of your life where you need to be more disciplined, such as physical health, mental health, organizational skills, eating, financial matters, family, and business dealings. What will you do to become more disciplined? Be specific.

■ Are there any things from a past race that you are still holding on to? If so, give them to the Lord today. Then, with your eyes fixed on Jesus, keep running.

Reading On

Isaiah 40:31   1 Corinthians 9:24

What Happens When We Die?

SCRIPTURE READING: Psalm 71:14-18

KEY VERSE: Psalm 71:18

Even when I am old and gray, do not forsake me,
my God, till I declare your power to the next generation,
your might to all who are to come.

As I get older, I think more and more about what comes next…I haven't yet formed a clear idea about what the hereafter might be like. I don't know if everyone's an angel, or an apparition. Or it's just all beyond comprehension. But I do hope that it's going to be better than here, because life on this planet is not exactly peaches and cream. I mean, this life is tough. I suppose that's the promise religion holds out. If you can take this life as it comes and give it your best, there will be something better afterwards.

I've always marveled at how belief in the hereafter gets accentuated as people grow older. Until their deathbeds, many of the great minds in science thought that because their soul and being were wrapped up in their body— the old ninety-eight cents' worth of chemicals—and that because after death these would no longer be a body, that was it. But now when they have to go, suddenly they want to believe in somebody up there because they don't know where they're going and they are scared.[18]

These thoughts of Lee Iacocca's touch on questions we all ask, and they can be boiled down to "What happens when we die?" Those of us who know the Lord have a better idea than the people around us who don't. And the psalmist who wrote today's Scripture passage understands the urgency of letting those folks know what we already know. The psalmist prays that God will not forsake him until he declares His power to the next generation. The psalmist knew he had work to do—and so do you and so do I.

In case you're not sure what that work is, read Jesus' command and promise in Matthew 28:19-20: "Go and make disciples of all nations, baptizing them in the name of the Father and of the Son and of the Holy Spirit, and teaching them to obey everything I have commanded you. And surely I am with you always, to the very end of the age."

We are commanded to share the news of sin and salvation. How well do you do that? Maybe it's hard for you to talk about your faith because you're unsure of the message. The following passages will help you brush up on the basics so you can be more confident as you talk about Jesus with people who don't know Him as their Lord and Savior.

- Romans 3:23
- Romans 6:23
- Acts 16:30-31
- Ephesians 2:8-9

- Romans 10:9-10
- John 10:28
- John 14:2-3

Once you've reviewed these truths, you can then invite the person you're sharing with to receive Christ by faith through a prayer like this one:

Lord Jesus, I need You. Thank You for dying on the cross for my sins. I open the door of my life and receive You as my Savior and Lord. Thank You for forgiving my sins and giving me eternal life. Take control of the throne of my life. Make me the kind of person You want me to be.[19]

Once this prayer has been prayed, the following passages offer assurance about life with Christ:

- Revelation 3:20
- Hebrews 13:5
- 1 John 5:11-13
- John 14:21

Those of us who know the Lord are commanded by Him to share the gospel with those who don't know Him. May we do so freely and boldly!

Father God, give me a passion for the message of Jesus Christ, the words and boldness I need to tell it, and an audience who wants to hear it. Holy Spirit, go before me to prepare hearts and help me when I have an opportunity to share the news of Jesus' life, death, and resurrection. Amen.

Taking Action

- If you've never walked through the process just outlined or prayed the prayer provided, kneel before God and ask Jesus to become the Lord of your life. Then read the scriptures listed to confirm your decision.

- If you've named Jesus Lord of your life, spend time practicing how you will share the good news with others. Know that sharing starts at home, and sharing happens in how we live, not just in what we say.

Reading On

Read the scriptures listed in today's devotion.

A High Calling

SCRIPTURE READING: Romans 12:9-21

KEY VERSE: Romans 12:9
*Love must be sincere. Hate what is evil;
cling to what is good.*

Dr. Halbeck, a missionary of the Church of England in the South of Africa, from the top of a neighboring hill saw lepers at work. He noticed two particularly, sowing peas in the field. One had no hands; the other had no feet—these members being wasted away by disease. The one who wanted the hands was carrying the other, who wanted the feet, upon his back; and he again carried the bag of seed, and dropped a pea every now and then, which the other pressed into the ground with his feet: and so they managed the work of one man between the two. Such should be the true union of the members of Christ's body, in which all the members should have the same care one for another.[20]

What a vivid and powerful picture of how the body of Christ is to function. Fundamental to that kind of unity is the love of Jesus. In today's reading, we are called to have a love that is "sincere." In many translations, Romans 12:9 reads, "Let love be without hypocrisy." The term *hypocrisy* is a stage term that means "acting a part." At the theater, we see people acting and pretending to be characters who aren't at all like who they are in real life. But in our walk of faith, we who are Christians are not to pretend to be someone we're not. Our love for one another is to be sincere, not an act of hypocrisy.

In today's passage, Paul gives other directives on how to live a Christian life that pleases and glorifies God. We are to choose the proper pathway in which to live. Here are some of those paths:

The Path of Sincerity (verse 9)
> Love must be sincere.
> Hate what is evil.
> Cling to what is good.

The Path of Humility (verse 10)
> Be devoted to one another in brotherly love.
> Honor one another above ourselves.

The Path of Passion (verses 11-12)
> Never lack in zeal.
> Keep fervent about serving the Lord.
> Be joyful in hope.
> Be patient in affliction.
> Be faithful in prayer.

The Path of Relationships (verses 13-20)
> Share with God's people who are in need.
> Practice hospitality.
> Bless those who persecute you.
> Do not curse those who hate you.
> Rejoice with those who rejoice.
> Mourn with those who mourn.
> Live in harmony with one another.
> Do not be proud.
> Be willing to associate with people of low position.
> Do not be conceited.
> Do not repay anyone evil for evil.
> Do what is right in the eyes of the Lord.
> Do not take revenge.
> If your enemy is hungry, feed him.

If your enemy is thirsty, give him something to drink.
Do not be overcome by evil, but overcome evil with
good.

God wants you and me to do all these things. No wonder I struggle every day to live the kind of life He wants me to live. In order to put these specifics into practice, I must read the Scripture and pray. Doing so helps me—and will help you—stand strong against Satan who would love to derail me from my goal of living a life that pleases and glorifies God.

Father God, here I am. Use me for Your kingdom. Teach me Your way of love. Fill me with Your love so that I may be willing to carry a brother or sister who needs my help—and help me to receive Your love when I need to be carried. It's a privilege to be called Your child. May I live a life worthy of that calling, a life that truly glorifies You. Amen.

Taking Action

- Choose six of the directives from the "paths" listed. Beside each one, note what you're going to do today and this week to live it out.

- Now write those six directives on an index card. Carry them with you as reminders of the goals you've set for yourself. Better yet, memorize them.

Reading On

Proverbs 6:16-19   Philippians 4:8

Meet Sergeant Major Pestretsov

SCRIPTURE READING: Ephesians 5:15-21

KEY VERSE: Ephesians 5:21
Submit to one another out of reverence for Christ.

Y ou've probably never heard of Nicolai Pestretsov, but now you may never forget him. He was 36 years old and a sergeant major in the Russian army stationed in Angola. His wife had traveled the long distance from home to visit her husband when, on an August day, South African military units entered the country in quest of black nationalist guerrillas taking sanctuary there. When the South Africans encountered the Russian soldiers, four people were killed. The rest of the Russians fled—except for Sergeant Major Pestretsov.

The South African troops captured Pestretsov, and a military communique explained the situation: "Sgt. Major Nicolai Pestretsov refused to leave the body of his slain wife, who was killed in the assault on the village. He went to the body of his wife and would not leave it, although she was dead."

What a picture of commitment! And what a series of questions it raises. Robert Fulghum, the teller of the story I read, asked these questions:

> Why didn't he run and save his own hide? What made him go back? Is it possible that he loved her? Is it possible that he wanted to hold her in his arms one last time? Is it possible that he needed to cry and grieve? Is it possible that he felt the stupidity of war? Is it possible that

he felt the injustice of fate? Is it possible that he thought of children, born or unborn? Is it possible that he didn't care what became of him now? Is it possible? We don't know. Or at least we don't know for certain. But we can guess. His actions answer.[21]

What do your actions say about your commitment to your spouse? What do your attitudes and your words reveal? Standing by the commitment you made before God and many witnesses when you said "I do" is key to standing by your wife.

Picture again Sergeant Major Pestretsov kneeling by the side of his wife's lifeless body, not wanting to leave the woman to whom he'd pledged his life. Even when his very life was at stake, he refused to leave. That is a high level of commitment, and we are to be just as committed to our wives. In fact, we who are married are to be as committed to our spouses as Christ is committed to the church He died for. Furthermore, as Christians, our marriages are to be witnesses to the world of Christ's love and grace. Clearly, marriage is not to be entered into casually.

In light of the importance God places on marriage, Emilie and I take very seriously the premarital counseling we do. We never, for instance, encourage two people to get married if one is a Christian and the other is not (2 Corinthians 6:14). A marriage needs to be rooted in each partner's commitment to love and serve the Lord or the union will be divided from the start because the two people will be looking in different directions. In addition, only a Christian marriage can result in a Christian home—a home that glorifies God and acts as His witness to the world.

> *Father God, it's sometimes difficult to stand by the commitment I've made to my spouse. I want to do my own thing my own way. Help me to stay true to the vow I made before You and other witnesses. Keep my love for my wife strong and powerful. Amen.*

Taking Action

- Today in your journal write out a fresh, new commitment to God and your spouse.

- Think back to your wedding day and review the vows you spoke. What do they mean to you today?

- In your marriage, what do you think it means to "submit to one another" in all things (Ephesians 5:21)?

- List five things you can do to show submission to your wife. Act on one of them today, and on the other four within the next month.

- Develop the habit of "reflexive giving"—of giving without being asked. Blessed are those who give automatically, and lucky are those who are married to them.

Reading On

Ephesians 5:22-33   Ephesians 6:10-18

Finding Contentment

Scripture reading: 1 Timothy 6:1-10

Key verse: 1 Timothy 6:6
Godliness with contentment is great gain.

I recall a special day many years ago when I was holding my grandson Bradley Joe Barnes II. As I rocked him in my arms, I found myself wondering what his life would be like as he grew to manhood. Would he achieve good grades and go to college? Would he enjoy and do well in sports? Would he be a fireman, a pastor, a teacher, a coach, a salesperson? Suddenly I realized that I was imagining what he could *do* when instead I could have been praying about who he would become.

Maybe you've found yourself focused on what you could be in the future rather than letting yourself be content in the present. I meet so many people who, unhappy in the present, are looking to the future—to the next paycheck, the next home, the next church, the next month, the next school, and, in some cases, the next marriage partner—to find peace and happiness. These people live with the hope that the future will bring the missing piece to their life, the piece that means contentment. I believe if you're not happy with what you have now, you'll never be satisfied with what you want.

Granted, it's not easy to be content. Our society works hard to make us aware of all that we don't have. The advertising industry often makes us want things we might not otherwise have considered. We can easily find ourselves drawn away from spiritual pursuits and instead be building our lives around reaching a certain financial goal, a specific level of possessions, or maybe a certain amount of vacation time. Simply put, we find ourselves putting our hope in wealth (1 Timothy 6:17).

As I sat there in Bradley's room, I began praying for all of his extended family, that each of us would help teach him to value what God values more than money, career, and fame. It's not that those are evil, but placing too high a value on them can lead to our downfall. "Those who want to get rich fall into temptation and a trap and into many foolish and harmful desires that plunge people into ruin and destruction" (1 Timothy 6:9).

As you read in today's passage, Paul learned that "godliness with contentment is great gain" (1 Timothy 6:6). When we find ourselves looking to the future because we aren't content with today, may God give us peace of mind and the ability to rest where He has placed us. May we pattern our lives after Christ and, walking in godliness, experience the rich blessing of contentment in the present.

> *Father God, You know that, like Paul, I want to be content in whatever circumstances I find myself. But You also know that too often I'm dissatisfied. Forgive me for valuing too highly those things that interfere with my pursuit of what You want for me and from me. You've given me so much! Thank You for those blessings. Teach me contentment, Lord. Amen.*

Taking Action

- Instead of being preoccupied with the challenging or oppressive circumstances of your life, start praising God for where you are.

- Ask God to reveal to you what He wants you to learn in your present situation.

- Write a letter to God thanking Him specifically for many of the ways He's blessed you. List the blessings individually.

Reading On

1 Timothy 6:11-21   Proverbs 22:1-2

It All Starts at Home

SCRIPTURE READING: Genesis 2:20-25

KEY VERSE: Genesis 2:23
*The man said, "This is now bone of my bones and
flesh of my flesh; she shall be called 'woman,'
for she was taken out of man."*

In his bestselling book *Straight Talk,* Lee Iacocca talks about the importance of the family:

> My father told me that the best way to teach is by example. He certainly showed me what it took to be a good person and a good citizen. As the old joke has it, "No one ever said on his deathbed, I should have spent more time on my business." Throughout my life, the bottom line I've worried about most was that my kids turn out all right.
>
> The only rock I know that stays steady, the only institution I know that works, is the family. I was brought up to believe in it—and I do. Because I think a civilized world can't remain civilized for long if its foundation is built on anything but the family. A city, state or country can't be any more than the sum of its vital parts—millions of family units. You can't have a country or a city or a state that's worth [anything] unless you govern within yourself in your day-to-day life.
>
> It all starts at home.[22]

In our Scripture reading today we are reminded that God Himself established the family. Although today's secular world is trying its hardest to downgrade the family as an institution, we know God will not abandon the good work He has begun in the family structure He created (Philippians 1:6).

The Bible is very clear in its teaching that woman was created for man; she is to be his helper. The Bible also clearly teaches that man and woman are designed for each other. These are key elements in God's plan for His people. Do you have a plan for your family? Have you and your mate taken time to determine what values you want to instill in your children and what guidelines you will give them as they grow?

Marriage causes a man to leave his mother and father, be united with his wife, and become one flesh with her. Is this a description of what has happened to you? Scripture then states, "Adam and his wife were both naked, and they felt no shame" (Genesis 2:25). Nakedness isn't always physical; it also includes emotional, spiritual, and psychological aspects of who we are. And one of the biggest challenges for Emilie and me is to stand before each other naked and unashamed. If we are following God's plans for our family, we can do just that.

Furthermore, we must follow God's plans for having a healthy family if, as Mr. Iacocca points out, we are to survive as a society. It does all start at home, so let's make it our goal to follow God's plan.

> *Father God, create in me a hunger to search out Your plan for my life and for my family. Give me the wisdom to major on the majors and not get sidetracked by the minors. It's easy to get distracted from Your plan, but I so want to follow Your master plan for me. When life is over I want You to say, "Well done, good and faithful servant." Help me today. Amen.*

Taking Action

- Meet with your mate and begin to prayerfully design a master plan for your family.

- Write this plan down and include specific goals for each family member.

- Begin today to raise good children who know and want to serve the Lord.

Reading On

Genesis 18:19

Getting Back to the Table

SCRIPTURE READING: Deuteronomy 6:1-9

KEY VERSES: Deuteronomy 6:6-7
*These commandments that I give you today are to be
on your hearts. Impress them on your children.
Talk about them when you sit at home and
when you walk along the road,
when you lie down and when you get up.*

Whatever happened to sitting down to the dinner table as a family—to good meals, no television, and talking about what happened in each person's day? Does this sound foreign to you? Are you thinking, *Get real! We're living in the twenty-first century. Life's not like it used to be?* Or perhaps you think encouraging the return to this tradition is your wife's domain. If so, you're missing out on having a great influence on your family's communication levels and their well-being.

If you can't imagine regular family meals, think how startled the early Shaker settlers would be if they visited in our homes for an evening. To help you imagine their reaction, read through the following rules the Shakers had in the 1800s for children's behavior at the table.

Advice to Children on Behavior at Table

First, in the morning, when you rise,
Give thanks to God, who well supplies
Our various wants, and gives us food,
Wholesome, nutritious, sweet, and good.

Then to some proper place repair,
And wash your hands and face with care;
And ne'er the table once disgrace
With dirty hands or dirty face.

When to your meals you have the call,
Promptly attend, both great and small;
Then kneel and pray, with closed eyes,
That God will bless these rich supplies.
When at the table you sit down,
Sit straight and trim, nor laugh nor frown;
Then let the elder first begin,
And all unite, and follow him.

Of bread, then take a decent piece,
Nor splash about the fat and grease;
But cut your meat both neat and square,
And take of both an equal share.
Also, of bones you'll take your due,
For bones and meat together grew.
If, from some incapacity,
With fat your stomach doesn't agree,
Or if you cannot pick a bone,
You'll please to let them both alone.

Potatoes, cabbage, turnip, beet,
And every kind of thing you eat,
Must neatly on your plate be laid,
Before you eat with pliant blade;
Nor ever—'tis an awkward matter,
To eat or sip out of the platter.

If bread and butter be your fare,
Or biscuit, and you find there are
Pieces enough, then take your slice,
And spread it over, thin and nice,
On one side, only; then you may
Eat in a decent, comely way.

Yet butter you must never spread
On nut-cake, pie, or dier-bread;
Or bread with milk,
Or bread with meat,
Butter with these you may not eat.
These things are all the best of food,
And need not butter to be good.

When bread or pie you cut or break,
Touch only what you mean to take;
And have no prints of fingers seen
On that that's left—nay, if they're clean.
Be careful, when you take a sip
Of liquid, don't extend your lip
So far that one may fairly think
That cup and all you mean to drink.

Then clean your knife—don't lick it, pray;
It is a nasty, shameful way—
But wipe it on a piece of bread,
Which snugly by your plate is laid.
Thus clean your knife, before you pass
It into plum or apple-sauce,
Or butter, which you must cut nice,
Both square and true as polish'd dice.

Cut not a pickle with a blade
Whose side with grease is overlaid;
And always take your equal share
Of coarse as well as luscious fare.
Don't pick your teeth, or ears, or nose,
Nor scratch your head, nor tonk your toes;
Nor belch nor sniff, nor jest nor pun,
Nor have the least of play or fun.

If you're oblig'd to cough or sneeze,
Your handkerchief you'll quickly seize,
And timely shun the foul disgrace

Of splattering either food or face.
Drink neither water, cider, beer,
With greasy lip or mucus tear;
Nor fill your mouth with food, and then
Drink, least you blow it out again.

And when you've finish'd your repast,
Clean plate, knife, fork—then, at the last,
Upon your plate lay knife and fork,
And pile your bones of beef and pork:
But if no plate, you may as well
Lay knife and fork both parallel.
Pick up your crumbs, and, where you eat,
Keep all things decent, clean, and neat.

Then rise, and kneel in thankfulness
To Him who does your portion bless;
Then straightly from the table walk,
Nor stop to handle things, nor talk.
If we mean never to offend,
To every gift we must attend,
Respecting meetings, work, or food,
And doing all things as we should.
Thus joy and comfort we shall find,
Love, quietness, and peace of mind;
Pure heavenly Union will increase,
And every evil work will cease.[23]

We don't have to go back to a list of rules this long or a list of rules of any length. But we do need to move back toward the family table. Today's Scripture passage—like the poem—challenges us to train our children. Instructions from the Lord are to be on our hearts. We are to impress them upon our children and talk about them when we walk along the road, when we lie down, and when we get up. What are you doing to properly train your children in all areas of life?

*Father God, once again You've reminded me of the enormous
privilege and responsibility of raising children. Give me energy,
patience, creativity, and perseverance to train my children so
that they will know You as their Lord and Savior and choose
to serve You. Amen.*

Taking Action

- Identify two or three areas of instruction for your children
  that you need to work on.

- What will you do to improve what you're doing for your
  children in each of those areas? What specific activities will
  help you strengthen a deficiency?

- Choose an evening to work on table manners. With
  your wife, plan an evening when the family can sit down
  together and enjoy a homemade meal. Depending on your
  kids' ages, get them involved choosing the menu, cooking,
  serving, clearing the table, and coming up with questions
  that the whole family can talk about. For instance, "What's
  the best thing that happened to you today?" As the leader
  of the family, don't leave manners, conversation skills, and
  politeness for your wife alone to teach.

Reading On

Psalm 127:1-5   Proverbs 22:6

Proverbs 1:1-7   Luke 12:22-34

It Has an Off Button

SCRIPTURE READING: 1 Corinthians 6:12-20

KEY VERSE: 1 Corinthians 6:12
"I have the right to do anything," you say—
but not everything is beneficial.

One great influence in our lives is the media. Unfortunately, most media in America is controlled by secular humanists, so the slant of a lot of print copy, programming, advertising, websites, and news portrays a secular worldview. Secular humanism is the view that mankind establishes his own moral values apart from the influence of anyone (including God), and he determines his destiny. He is the "master of his own fate."

The problem with such a life view is that it has no absolutes. Everything is relative. There is no external or eternal reference point. We can make up our own rules as we go. How do we know if sexual promiscuity is immoral or not? Why shouldn't we cheat in business? Why should family life be valued higher than careers?

Through broadcast media and advertising, which relies heavily on subliminal suggestion, we are consciously and unconsciously lured to want things we don't have. We are encouraged to wish we lived different lives. The secrets of fanning our smoldering desires and wants has been elevated to a scientific level. The economic goal of television is, after all, to sell products and services.

Perhaps the only way to overcome this dilemma is to reevaluate our sources of entertainment and information. Personally, I have stopped watching television, and I am reading more books.

First Corinthians 6:12 (NASB) offers us a credo worth adopting: "All things are lawful for me, but not all things are profitable. All things are lawful for me, but I will not be mastered by anything" My concern is that my unconscious mind will be mastered in an area in which I have little or no ability to resist. Our unconscious minds have no walls around them and no sentinel at the gate.

Watch television commercials one evening or pay attention to how many ads pop up on your computer screen. Have you been shaping your life to fit the images impressed on you by these ads? The life the ads are selling loves pleasure and sensuality, doesn't deny itself anything, and has a right to whatever goal it sets. Have you started to make decisions based on this version of existence? Does this represent any part of you these days?

Remember the heroes you grew up with? They were probably men of adventure, honor, and justice. Unfortunately, the prime-time heroes of contemporary society are shaped by the creative penmanship of morally bankrupt humanists. Frankly, I believe they represent a minority view. Many great examples of genuine accomplishment, faith, and courage abound, but they are supplanted by the neutered characters promoted by media owners and participants.

Don't we want the models for our children to be people who have sacrificed and contributed to the betterment of life—famous scientists, artists, thinkers, missionaries, statesmen, builders, and other heroes and saints? They are out there, but we're not going to find them through mainstream media.[24]

Patrick Morley gives us a lot to think about in this excerpt from his book *The Man in the Mirror*: The insidious power of television is destroying our family life. As men, we have to take control of what we allow to come into our homes. We'd call the police if a burglar entered our homes and stole something of value—and that is what television is doing. As our key verse today teaches, what is permissible is not always beneficial. That is a warning to heed when we're considering the power of television.

Think about the role the television plays in your home. Are you or your family members addicted to television? Can you go a week without having the television on? Try it and see what happens. If nerves are on edge, tempers are flaring, and people are angry, these could be signs that you're too dependent on television for entertainment and escape. As the head of the family, take the lead in getting this stealer of time under control.

> *Father God, You know I want the best for me and my family. I want to protect them from all that would hurt and rob them. Make me aware of those things that steal from us. Give me the courage to be strong in this and, if necessary, turn off the television in our home. Amen.*

Taking Action

- Evaluate the amount of time you and/or your family watch television. What kinds of programs do you watch? If they are sending false messages about life, you may want to develop an alternate plan for using your time more effectively.

- What could you and your family do instead of watching television? Here are some ideas: go to a play or a concert; have a picnic; watch family videos; read books; listen to good music; talk together about life, the day-to-day and the big picture; take a walk; exercise; jog; or swim. Choose one to do this weekend and a second to do next weekend.

- What can you, as the head of the home, do to build up the family when so much of society is trying to tear it down? What activities can you plan?

Reading On

Ephesians 4:29   1 Corinthians 10:23-24

What You Teach

Scripture reading: Daniel 1:1-21

Key verse: Daniel 1:8
*Daniel resolved not to defile himself with the royal
food and wine, and he asked the chief official
for permission not to defile himself this way.*

Many of us have taught our children to look both ways before crossing the street, to be courteous and respectful, to say their prayers, and to honor God and their families. But have we instilled in them the virtues and values that will help them refuse to participate in things that go against God and defile their bodies or minds?

In the book of Daniel we see a son who was raised by the teachings found in Leviticus 11. Daniel did not want to defile his body by eating foods that were unclean or had been offered to pagan idols before being put on the king's table. (Eating food offered to a pagan god was an indication of loyalty to that god.)

Notice the deep commitment of faith that enabled Daniel to take the stands he took. He bore testimony to the faithfulness of parents and mentors and leaders who taught him the central issues of obedience to biblical principles. Because of this, Daniel was able to withstand the forces he faced in a hostile land. But since he was captured by the Babylonians and taken from his Israeli homeland, his parents may never have known the results of his early training in their home.

Teaching future generations about faith, conviction, and faithfulness to God is the most important part of our legacy as fathers, grandfathers, and mentors. We might not live to see how our children or grandchildren will respond as adults, but our commitment should never waver. Our job is to raise and prepare our children and the next generation for God's calling.

> *Father God, at times I become so discouraged as a father because I sound like a squeaky wheel around my children and family. But You know that I want the very best for them. I want them to know of Your love for them, to live a disciplined life, to be responsible for their actions, and to have a healthful selection of nourishment for their bodies and souls. Thank You for putting these desires in my heart. Give me the courage and strength to follow You and follow through. Amen.*

Taking Action

- Do you have a plan to raise your children or to encourage your grandchildren? What do you want them to become? How are they going to get there?

- Are you raising your children so they can think for themselves, or are you still making all their decisions for them? Cut the cord early.

- What areas of your life do you want to change so that your children are better equipped to face adulthood? What are you going to do to get there?

Reading On

Leviticus 11	Hebrews 11:23-28
Luke 2:41-52	Exodus 34:15

Wisdom's Source

SCRIPTURE READING: James 3:13-18

KEY VERSE: James 3:13 NASB

Who among you is wise and understanding?
Let him show by his good behavior his
deeds in the gentleness of wisdom.

I have an identical twin brother named Bill. When my children, Jennifer and Bradley, were very young and couldn't tell my brother and me apart, they would refer to us as the "two daddies." When our grandchildren arrived, they also were confused when we were together. They called us the "two papas."

That's the way it is with wisdom. Both kinds are called by the same name of "wisdom," but they are different. In fact, the two wisdoms come from different sources, have different means, and most definitely have different ends. James talks about these two wisdoms in chapter 3, verse 15 of his letter:

- one comes from above
- one is earthly, natural, and demonic

The one that comes from above is…

- pure
- peaceable
- gentle
- reasonable

- full of mercy
- full of good fruits
- unwavering (verse 17)

The second wisdom produces…

- bitter jealousy
- selfish ambition
- arrogance
- hypocrisy (verses 14,17)

Notice the difference in the fruit that each produces:

- The first produces the fruit of righteousness and peace (verse 18)
- The second produces the fruit of disorder and every evil thing (verse 16)

Wouldn't it be nice to have godly wisdom and youth at the same time? Life, however, doesn't work that way. We partner with God throughout our lives, and wisdom comes from Him and from our experiences as we encounter His faithfulness and our own weaknesses. The fruit of wisdom that comes from God is great, and I guarantee that it is worth the wait.

Father God, I don't always like the aged face that reflects back to me in the morning through the mirror. But my friends and family tell me that I have wisdom and the ability to share it. It doesn't seem fair that the two must go together. It seems like the world is drowning in knowledge, but we are starved for wisdom. Let me stand back and look at the real priorities of life. I don't want to chase rainbows that have no pot of gold at the end. Let me tell the difference. I want to say no to merely good things and save my yes for the very best. Amen.

Taking Action

- Which of the two wisdoms do you want to pursue?

- Meditate on your actions and see if they produce the right kind of fruit. If not, why not? What needs to be changed?

- Make a contract with a friend who will hold you accountable to produce the fruit of peace and righteousness.

Reading On

Proverbs 4:5-7   Proverbs 9:10

1 Corinthians 2:6-13

The Blessing of Relationships

SCRIPTURE READING: Ecclesiastes 4:8-12

KEY VERSE: Ecclesiastes 4:12 NASB

A cord of three strands is not quickly torn apart.

M any times we look to others to help us out, and we complain when we don't receive the help we think we deserve. But help starts within ourselves and then moves outward. We need to take an inventory of all the skills and tools God has so graciously given us at birth. We tend to take for granted those attributes of success that were given to us at the very beginning of our lives. In addition, King Solomon in all his wisdom told us that friends are great blessings to our family. He emphasized this in Ecclesiastes chapter 4:

- Two are better than one because they have a good return for their labor (verse 9).
- Woe to the one who falls when there is not another to lift him up (verse 10).
- If two lie down together they keep warm (verse 11).
- Two can resist one who tries to overpower them (verse 12).
- A cord of three strands is not quickly torn apart (verse 12).

Are you working on relationships that build these kinds of blessings? Begin at home with your family members. Throughout Scripture we are told to be united with one another. Unity should be our goal as husband and wife, parent and child, or child and sibling.

Begin to develop the traits that have eternal worth, not the temporal traits that last for such a short time.

In Ecclesiastes 4:8 (NASB) Solomon presents one of the most basic questions of life: "For whom am I laboring and depriving myself of pleasure?" Is it all for vanity? Does it have redeeming value to you and your family? If not, do something about it.

> *Father God, in my heart and soul I want my family to be a blessing to me, and likewise I want to be a blessing to them. At times it seems to be in vain. Bring to mind those traits that are so important for friendships. I do want to be counted as a friend to those around me. Let me be a discerning person when it comes to doing my best for the people You have placed in my life. Let me major on major issues and minor on minor issues of life. Amen.*

Taking Action

- If you are married, discuss this question with your wife: "For whom am I laboring and depriving myself of pleasure?"

- What kind of friend are you?

- What qualities do you look for in a friend? Whom would you consider your best friend? Why?

- Would you have wanted someone like yourself as a father? Why or why not?

- Whom do you feel very comfortable around? Why?

Reading On

Proverbs 18:24	John 15:13
James 4:4	1 John 1:7

Will You Be the One?

SCRIPTURE READING: Joshua 1:1-9

KEY VERSE: Joshua 1:9 NASB

Have I not commanded you? Be strong and courageous! Do not tremble or be dismayed, for the LORD your God is with you wherever you go.

Once upon a time all the mice met together in council and discussed the best means of protecting themselves against the attacks of the cat. After several suggestions had been debated, a mouse of some standing and experience got up and said, "I think I have hit upon a plan which ensures our safety in the future, provided you approve it and carry it out. It is that we should fasten a bell around the neck of our enemy the cat, which will by its tinkling warn us of her approach."

This proposal was warmly applauded, and it had already been decided to adopt it when an old mouse finally got up on his feet and said, "I agree with you all that the plan before us is an admirable one, but I ask: Who is going to bell the cat?"

—Adapted from Aesop's Fables

Wouldn't it be wonderful if all we had to do in order to be brave is to talk about it? But true courage and bravery require action. Our society is starving for people with courage. We look for our heroes in sports, politics, movies, business, and church, but many of them fail the test. We hunger for the character trait of courage, but few people are able to deliver on it.

Will you be the one to follow decision with action? Would you be the one to bell the cat?

As parents we are continually tested by the decisions we must make. Are we able to stand alone and make hard decisions on what we as a family are going to do? It's difficult to be in the minority as a friend, a neighbor, or a parent—to just say no. Unfortunately, the greatest pressure often comes from those we love the most!

Joshua had a similar dilemma, but he stood tall and delivered this statement:

> If it is disagreeable in your sight to serve the Lord,
> choose for yourselves today whom you will serve:
> whether the gods which your fathers served which
> were beyond the River, or the gods of the Amorites in
> whose land you are living; but as for me and my house,
> we will serve the Lord (Joshua 24:15 nasb).

Joshua was willing to stand up and be heard. He had the courage to bell the cat. Are you facing a similar difficulty in your life? If so, look to God to find the answer. He says He will never leave us or forsake us. That is a promise we can take to the bank.

We have some friends in Northern California who have made a valor ribbon for each of their two sons. When the parents are aware that the sons have taken some action that requires courage, bravery, or valor, they recognize this fact by letting the boys wear their ribbon that evening at home. It might be for...

- not smoking, drinking, or taking drugs when someone offers them,
- not cheating on a test when the opportunity arises to do so,

- saying no to premarital sex,
- returning found money, or
- assisting someone who is in need of help.

These parents recognize the importance of praising their sons' acts of courage.

Our reading today states,

- The law of Scripture shall not depart from your mouth.
- You shall meditate on it day and night.
- Be careful to do according to all that is written in it.
- This will make your way prosperous.
- You will have success.
- Be strong and courageous.
- Do not tremble or be dismayed.
- The Lord your God is with you wherever you go (Joshua 1:8-9 NASB).

Let us not only talk the talk but also walk the walk, for God is always with us and we are never alone.

> *Father God, oh how I want to have courage enough to stand up and be counted in difficult situations. I really want to have the courage to bell the cat. Support me as I stand strong with my convictions. Don't let me waver as I stand tall. Let those around me gain strength from my strength, which I receive from You. Let me not only believe the gospel but also behave the gospel. Amen.*

Taking Action

- In what areas of your life do you need to show courage? What are you going to do about those situations?

- You see a way to get a good deal or a leg up, but it hurts another person. Do you move forward, ignoring the consequence to another, or do you step back and figure out a better solution?

- The bank ATM gives you $60 instead of the $20 you asked for. What will you do?

- If you knew that a neighbor was abusing his wife and/or children, what would you do?

Reading On

Isaiah 41:10   Deuteronomy 33:27

Psalm 118:17   Philippians 4:13

Humbled and Blessed

SCRIPTURE READING: Luke 1:46-56

KEY VERSE: Luke 1:52

He has brought down rulers from their
thrones but has lifted up the humble.

In the New Testament, we find the word "humility" to mean a personal quality of dependence on God and respect for other people. It is not a natural human instinct, but a God-given virtue acquired through holy living.

While the mind of the natural man is selfish and proud, the essence of Jesus' mind is unselfish and loving toward others. Christ was our great example of a proper walk—pleasing to God.

Our hearts must be transformed by the Holy Spirit so that we can reflect God's love to others through the humble example of Jesus.

Corrie ten Boom, an unbelievable Dutch woman who survived the horror of World War II while in the confines of a German death camp, received a lot of praise for what she did during her confinement, and yet she remained unfazed by all the tributes. When asked how she managed to stay so humble among all these honors, she humbly replied, "I accept every compliment as a flower and say thank you, and each evening I put them in a bunch and lay them at Jesus' feet, where the praise belongs."

Our world is full of men and women who are eager to take God's honor and heap it on their own heads. But God has a way of humbling us. From my own experience in life I know that I need to come before His throne with open arms and humbly bow before Him, seeking whatever He has for my life. We all need to learn this lesson of humility in life because God has promised that if we don't humble ourselves, He will do it for us.

The Greek culture of the first century despised the quality of humility, but Jesus entered the world as a humble Savior. He became obedient to God's will, which led to His death on the cross. Throughout Jesus' walk on this earth He taught people to be humble before God and man.

In today's passage we see that God will exalt those who are humble. Humility comes from God and results in the praise of God.

Father God, You know how I want to lay down a gathering of compliments at Your feet and give You all the praise. I know I am nothing without You. You have taken me, an ordinary man, and exalted me to a point at which I don't feel adequate. Thank You for fulfilling Your promise in me. Through my life may You be richly praised and lifted up. I am humbled that You can use me in life. Let me touch people so they know they have seen and felt Jesus. And may I always give You the glory among men. Amen.

Taking Action

- Ask God for a heart of humility daily.

- Where in your life do you hold on to pride and ego? Consider how to change with the Lord's help.

- Ask a friend to share with you those areas of your life where you need specific rearranging. This act of humility can lead to great growth. Caring friends can hold us with compassion as they point out our blind spots.

Reading On

James 4:10   Colossians 2:18

1 Peter 5:6   Romans 5:15

Trading Our Thoughts for His

SCRIPTURE READING: Isaiah 55:6-13

KEY VERSE: Isaiah 55:8
*"For my thoughts are not your thoughts,
neither are your ways my ways," declares the LORD.*

What if anyone at any time could examine your thoughts—past or present? That would be scary and convicting for most of us! Compared to the thoughts of God, our human ponderings seem so frail and flawed. I can't imagine being exposed for the lowliness of my thought life.

Sometimes I question, "God, why did You permit that plane to crash, or why was it necessary for that trial to take place?" I want to crawl inside God's mind and see how it functions and how He thinks. Then I realize that He is the potter and I am the clay. His thoughts are so much higher than mine.

I am awestruck when I consider the viewpoint our all-knowing, all-seeing God has of our hearts and of the world as a whole. And I am grateful when I recognize the gift Scripture gives to us by offering us insight into God's character and His desire for our thought process.

In Philippians 4:8 Paul gives us an idea of what God calls us to dwell on. With a reasonable list that even I can manage, Paul guides us to think on these things:

- whatever is true
- whatever is noble

- whatever is right
- whatever is pure
- whatever is lovely
- whatever is admirable

If there is any excellence and if anything worthy of praise, let your mind dwell on these things. Then in verse 9, he gives us some action steps:

- Whatever you have learned, received, heard, or seen in me—
- put it into practice.
- And the God of peace will be with you.

As Christians we are all models that people watch to see what God is like. They are watching and hearing what we have to say about life. Either they accept our level of thought or they reject it by what they have learned, received, heard, and seen in us.

We want to be reflections of God. As people see us in action, do they see what this Christian walk is all about? Do our children and those around us ask, "Have I ever seen a Christian?" Or do they know absolutely that they have seen a Christian when they look at us?

If people were to stumble across a collection of our thoughts, what would they truly find? What would they discover that was honorable about our inner workings? What would they discover to be dishonorable or deceptive?

The more we search our own hearts and minds and give the less-than-holy findings to God, the more we are able to walk, act, think, relate, communicate, and share with others from a transformed mind.

Father God, thank You for challenging me in this area of

thoughts. Let me focus on pure thoughts that will stimulate me to be more Christlike. When I have a choice between two levels of thought, give me the strength and courage to take the higher road. Help the men who read today's thoughts to be challenged to think on the good things of life. May we all raise our level of thought. Amen.

Taking Action

Evaluate your thought life.

- Where are the stumbling blocks?

- What do you like about your thought life?

- What do you want to change?

- How will you change?

Reading On

Galatians 5:19-21	Psalm 94:11
Galatians 5:22-23	Matthew 15:16-20

Planning Your Days

SCRIPTURE READING: Matthew 6:25-34

KEY VERSE: Matthew 6:33
*"Seek first his kingdom and his righteousness,
and all these things will be given to you as well."*

We live in an anxious society. Many of us are more worried about tomorrow than today. We bypass all of today's contentment because of our worry about what might happen tomorrow. In our passage today we read that the early Christians asked the same basic questions (verse 31):

- What shall we eat?
- What shall we drink?
- What shall we wear?

Jesus tells them in verse 34, "Do not worry about tomorrow, for tomorrow will worry about itself. Each day has enough trouble of its own." He gives them a formula for establishing the right priorities of life in verse 33: "Seek first his kingdom and his righteousness, and all these things will be given to you as well." To use this verse as our mission verse, Emilie and I daily claim these two instructions:

- Seek His kingdom.
- Seek His righteousness.

When we seek these two things we find that our day takes shape, and we can say yes we will do that, or no we will not do that. Often we are overwhelmed by having too many things to do. Life offers many good choices on how to schedule our time. But we all have only 24 hours a day. How are we to use those hours effectively?

When we begin to set priorities, we determine what is important and what isn't, and we decide how much time we are willing to give each activity.

The Bible gives us guidelines for the godly ordering of our lives. Adopting God's priorities helps us know how and when to use our resources. We cannot do all the things that come our way. Emilie and I have a motto that helps us when we face too many choices and requests: "Say no to the good things and save each yes for the best."

Don't be afraid to say no. If you have established Matthew 6:33 as one of the key verses in your life, you can quickly decide whether a particular opportunity will help you to seek God's kingdom and His righteousness.

After learning to say no easily, you can begin to major on the big things of life and not get bogged down with issues that don't really matter.

> *Father God, since You are a God of order, I also want to have order in my life. Thank You for sharing this verse with our family many years ago. It has certainly helped us to major on the majors and to minor on the minor issues of life. May other men get excited about not being anxious for tomorrow and realize that You take care of our daily needs. Amen.*

Taking Action

- Look in the mirror and say no ten times. Do this every day for a week.

- Memorize Matthew 6:33 and share it with others.

- Each morning write out a to-do list. After each activity write yes or no. Then follow through on these decisions.

- Rank each yes in order of importance. (Let the most important one be number 1.)

- Cross off each activity as you get it accomplished.

Reading On

Psalm 119:105	1 Corinthians 14:40
Psalm 32:8	Luke 5:15-16

Do all the good you can,
By all the means you can,
In all the ways you can,
In all the places you can,
At all the times you can,
To all the people you can,
As long as ever you can.

—JOHN WESLEY

Notes

1. Charles R. Swindoll and Lee Hough, *You and Your Child* (Nashville: Thomas Nelson Publishers, 1977), a study guide to accompany a series of topics on this subject, 1993, 33.

2. Adapted from Stephen R. Covey, *The Seven Habits of Highly Effective People* (New York: Simon and Schuster, 1989).

3. June Hunt, *Seeing Yourself Through God's Eyes* (Grand Rapids, MI: Zondervan Publishing House, 1989), 33.

4. Ed and Carol Neuenschwander, *Two Friends in Love* (Portland, OR: Multnomah Press, 1986), 175.

5. Robert Fulghum, *All I Really Need to Know I Learned in Kindergarten* (New York: Ballantine Books, 1986), 4-6.

6. Lee Iacocca, *Talking Straight* (New York: Bantam Books, 1988), 27.

7. Dr. R. Newton, *6000 Sermon Illustrations,* ed. Elon Foster (Grand Rapids, MI: Baker Book House, 1992), 286.

8. Gigi Graham Tchividjian, *Women's Devotional Bible,* NIV (Grand Rapids, MI: The Zondervan Corporation, 1990), 1307.

9. Bruce Narramore, *You're Someone Special* (Grand Rapids, MI: The Zondervan Corporation, 1978), adapted from 61-62.

10. Stu Weber, *Tender Warrior* (Sisters, OR: Multnomah Books, 1993), adapted from 54-57.

11. Newton, *6000 Sermon Illustrations,* 286.

12. Fulghum, *All I Really Need to Know,* 4-6.

13. Alan Loy McGinnis, *The Friendship Factor* (Minneapolis, MN: Augsburg, 1979), 23.

14. Gary J. Oliver, "Black-and-White Living in a Gray World" in Bill Bright, et al., *Seven Promises of a Promise Keeper* (Colorado Springs, CO: Focus on the Family Publishing, 1994).

15. Ibid., 85-90.

16. Ibid.

17. Based on Jerry Kirk's contribution in Bill Bright, et al., *Seven Promises of a Promise Keeper.*

18. Iacocca, *Talking Straight,* 69.

19. Bill Bright, *Four Spiritual Laws* (San Bernardino, CA: Campus Crusade for Christ, Inc., 1965), 10.

20. Newton, *6000 Sermon Illustrations,* 309.

21. Fulghum, *All I Really Need to Know I Learned in Kindergarten,* 29-31.

22. Iacocca, *Talking Straight,* 17.

23. "Advice to Children on Behavior at Table," *The Manifesto,* April 1898.

24. Adapted from Patrick Morley, *The Man in the Mirror* (Brentwood, TN: Wolgemuth and Hyatt, 1989), 12-14.

About the Author

Bob Barnes lives life to the fullest. Throughout his years of work in education, business, and ministry, he's enjoyed many opportunities to serve people. Retirement affords him more time to encourage his family, friends, men, and the people who read his books. While this former farm boy is grateful for time spent working in the yard and garden, his favorite pastime is doing anything with Emilie, his partner in life and ministry.

After more than 50 years of marriage, Bob and Emilie still thoroughly enjoy one another's company while reading, going for walks, attending church and a small-group Bible study, and watching movies while sharing a bowl of popcorn. Together they inspire their kids, grandkids, and great-granddaughter by modeling a life of faith, joy, and commitment.

For more information about Bob and Emilie Barnes,
their books, and their ministry, please send a
self-addressed, stamped envelope to:

More Hours in My Day
2150 Whitestone Drive
Riverside, CA 92506

or email:
Sheri@EmilieBarnes.com

More Great Harvest House Books
by Bob Barnes

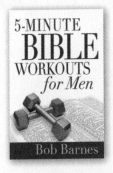

5-Minute Bible Workouts for Men

Is the pressure getting to you? Are you looking for relief? With demands that constantly call for your attention, it's easy to procrastinate or skip reading the Bible or praying. But spending time with God is the best stress-reducer there is! So grab five minutes a day and use these devotions filled with valuable direction, biblical wisdom, and encouragement that will renew and revive your spirit.

Start your day with a one-on-one workout with God. Let Him fill you with peace and energy all day long.

5-Minute Faith Builders for Men

Can you use a pick-me-up? Do you need something to help keep you going? Discover God's wisdom for your life in these brief and powerful devotions from Bob Barnes. With his trademark down-to-earth style, he encourages you to use God's Word as your guiding force, develop a powerful prayer life that is rich and real, lead your family based on biblical principles, and walk joyfully with God every day.

An Old Guy's Guide to Living Young

Would you like to know the secrets to a vibrant, faith-filled life? Bob Barnes enthusiastically shares his knowledge, wisdom, and insights to help you get more out of life. Drawing from his experiences as a husband, respected patriarch, businessman, author, and man of faith, Bob provides brief, inspiring chapters about how you can

- let hope permeate your circumstances and perspective
- devote your days to God with discipline and commitment
- create a legacy through compassionate and generous living

Capture the life-transforming attitudes, actions, and priorities that will increase your faith, build your quality of life, benefit the people you love, and create a lasting legacy for the next generations.

■ ■ ■ ■ ■ ■

To learn more about other books by Bob and Emilie Barnes and to read sample chapters, log on to our website:
www.HarvestHousePublishers.com

HARVEST HOUSE PUBLISHERS
EUGENE, OREGON